Technical Writing for Software Developers

Enhance communication, improve collaboration, and leverage AI tools for software development

Chris Chinchilla

Technical Writing for Software Developers

Group Product Manager: Kunal Sawant

Publishing Product Manager: Akash Sharma

Project Manager: Prajakta Naik

Book Project Manager: Manisha Singh

Senior Editor: Rounak Kulkarni

Technical Editor: Jubit Pincy

Copy Editor: Safis Editing

Proofreader: Rounak Kulkarni

Indexer: Hemangini Bari

Production Designer: Prafulla Nikalje

Senior Developer Relations Marketing Coordinator: Shrinidhi Monaharan

Business Development Executive: Kriti Sharma

First published: March 2024

Production reference: 01220324

Published by Packt Publishing Ltd.

Grosvenor House

11 St Paul's Square

Birmingham

B3 1RB, UK.

ISBN 978-1-83508-040-5

www.packtpub.com

To everyone in the many tech-writing communities I am involved in. Keep up the good work.

Contributors

About the author

Chris Chinchilla is a technical writer, blogger, video maker, and podcaster with over ten years of experience. He has worked on numerous large and small technical projects and products, helping them explain what they have built to the outside world. He is active in many tech writing and non-tech writing communities, helping mentor new writers. He maintains a handful of open source tools to help writers create the best words they can. In his spare time, he writes games, fiction, and interactive fiction.

About the reviewers

As an experienced technical writer and community leader, **Segun Light Ige-Olumide** is passionate about empowering developers and fostering growth within the tech industry. With five years of experience, he creates engaging content that addresses developers' evolving needs. Segun has also led multiple successful developer communities, prioritizing collaboration, learning, and professional development. Committed to making a meaningful impact, he strives to contribute to the tech community's ongoing growth and innovation.

Fortune Ikechi is a software engineer and technical writer with extensive experience in enhancing developer relations and community engagement. His commitment to innovation and community building and his ability to bridge the gap between developers and products have driven product adoption and awareness. Being a tech community advocate, Fortune continues to share his expertise and insights, contributing to a better understanding of technology's potential.

Table of Contents

6

Selecting the Right Tools for Efficient Documentation Creation　　65

7

Handling Other Content Types for Comprehensive Documentation　　87

8

Collaborative Workflows with Automated Documentation Processes   105

9

Opportunities to Enhance Documentation with AI Tools   119

Preface

Documentation is fundamental to helping potential and current users understand the amazing projects you build. For many developers and other technical-minded people, documentation is a challenging chore. *Technical Writing for Software Developers* covers all the important points you need to know to make great documentation easier and suited to developer workflows and tools.

Welcome, wordsmiths!

Before I begin, I'd like to start where I always like to begin, with some history.

My grandfather worked for a long-since-acquired company that created and laid submarine cables, the long and large network of cables lurking under the sea that enable communications between countries worldwide. When he laid them from the back of the large ships that ran between the UK and Canada, he was laying gigantic reams of copper wires mostly meant for telephone and telegram traffic. By the time he retired, the internet existed in some rudimentary form, telephones were widespread, and he gave me a nugget of advice that I still remember today, despite being too young to really understand what he meant:

"Optic fibers are the future."

And he was right. Now, there are more submarine cables than ever, shuttling petabytes of data back and forth per day. Our work and play rely so much on a relatively small amount of vulnerable wires that rest on the ocean bed, are prone to damage and attack, and have disconnected smaller nations from the world.

I digress. Why am I telling you this in a book about tech writing?

My grandfather started his professional career as a technical artist. He drew up plans and instructions on how to make and lay these essential cables, plus how to use the machinery needed for the task. I can't imagine he ever anticipated much of the work you and I do now (he died in 2001), but I could imagine that he would be amused that we ended up in related careers and fascinated by some of the projects I have worked on.

My point is that if we consider "technical writing" to mean explaining something to someone else so they can understand it and how to use it to accomplish their goals, then "technical writing" is everywhere.

What is technical writing?

Safety instructions, appliance, and furniture manuals, online tutorials and guides, books, technical blogs, high-risk equipment installation instructions, and even board game manual instructions are forms of technical writing.

This book is aimed at software developers who want to learn how to explain better what they build. It doesn't intend to cover all the examples above. However, as with many complex topics, sometimes it's important to understand how we got where we are today and the gamut of related work that others undertake. My grandfather was also more of an engineer at heart at a time when qualifications were more necessary but harder to get if you came from a poor family like he did. But he was passionate about helping those around him understand complex technical topics. One of his proudest moments was captured in a tattered old black and white photo of him explaining how the cables worked to a young Prince Phillip (the last English Queen's husband). I studied computer science and spent several years in development teams before realizing I enjoyed explaining technical topics more. In short, you're in good company!

Ok, I've explained what technical writing is, but that doesn't always help. Sometimes, when figuring out what's expected or typical in a role or task, it's easier to look at what it doesn't include.

What technical writing doesn't include?

I should say that many of these potential tasks depend on the team's size. As possibly the only person on a team or project with the ability or desire to communicate and explain, you may find yourself called to undertake tasks you never anticipated. You might be OK with doing them all, and that's OK. But maybe you're not OK or don't have the time and the inclination, and that's also OK. What I present in this section attempts to get to the core of what technical writing work should be, so you shouldn't feel you *have* to do any of the other work.

Technical writing isn't copywriting

Many people you speak to hear "writing" and think you want to edit their website copy or other assorted text tweaks. Depending on the topic and the project size, you may still be interested, and the best-suited for the task, but technical writing is generally specialized and requires niche technical knowledge. In short, you're probably not the most suited and are too expensive for the job.

Technical writing isn't interface copy

I have worked on some teams where technical writers *handle the text that appears* on buttons and in **Command Line Interface (CLI)** commands, and for a product aimed at developers, it can make sense. However, there are probably people more suited to the task whom you can instead advise.

Technical writing isn't blogging

I need to be careful here. I blog *a lot* because I like blogging, and there is also great demand from marketing departments at technical companies for people who understand the technology to help them spread that word to other technically minded people. Marketing teams will be very happy if you do want to blog, but it doesn't suit everyone, and you don't have to feel obligated.

Technical writing isn't tech journalism

This is another one where I don't help as I also run my own podcast, reporting on events and interviewing people in the tech industry. A technical background has helped me a lot with some subjects, and learning to write more clearly has also helped me produce clearer content. However, most tech journalists I encounter aren't that technical, and I have frequently taken issue with the level of misunderstanding in some tech reporting and feel that we should consider much of what we call "tech journalism" to be more "consumer journalism". I doubt many of you reading this book will be asked to tackle any tech journalism, but surprisingly, it's what many think of when you mention "technical writing".

Technical writing isn't marketing copy

Technical writers are often shuffled back and forth within the corporate structure and occasionally become part of marketing teams. However, technical writing should only cover facts (more on that in *Chapter 4, Page Structure and How It Aids Reading*), and you shouldn't ever feel compelled to write press releases or any other pure marketing copy.

A technical writing definition

Technical writing is any media, mostly words, but not always, that explains to someone how something works and how they can use it. This could be as little as a README file, code comments, or as much as pages and pages of tutorials and reference material. I laid out what tasks I consider to be outside of that definition, but some are more outside of it than others, and if there's one piece of advice to take away from this section, it's this. Your task is to find the best way to explain complex topics. You will learn through this book and, over time on your own, the best ways to do this that work for you and your audience.

Who am I?

Hey there! That last section told you a little about me, but my name is Chris Ward. More typically known online as "Chris Chinchilla," as my real name is so common in English that no one would ever find me. At the time of writing, I live in Berlin. However, I was born in London and spent a long time in Melbourne. I have a degree in Multimedia Computer Science. After completing my studies, I played in bands for a few years before settling into the classic programmer job of the early 2000s, building websites for early e-commerce businesses. I built many of these sites in Drupal, which exposed me to open source software. Drupal was quite ahead of its time in many ways, especially when it came to the community. I enjoy programming, but I realized relatively quickly in my career that I don't quite have the mindset to be an *excellent* programmer. At Drupal community events, there were often activities for people who don't code, and I started contributing by summarizing issue discussions and writing documentation. I was much better at this and had never realized it was a job people would pay you to do! Over the years after that, I moved in and out of technology ecosystems and between roles in tech writing and editing, tech blogging, developer relations, and more. Also, typically, I have a couple of side projects along the way.

Who can learn from this book?

People who are good at explaining topics often sit between and have experience in different disciplines and roles. A good tech writer often has engineering, support, design, product, and marketing exposure and can help bring insights between these teams. In short, no matter your experience or your journey to get that experience, if you are keen to help people understand, then technical writing is the place for you!

This book is mostly aimed at developers who want to learn how to explain their creations to the world better. However, anyone involved with a technical product can find something useful here. And for any of you reading who are already writing documentation, welcome! I think you will also find enough new information to make this book worthwhile reading, especially from *Chapter 7*, *Handling Other Content Types for Comprehensive Documentation* onwards.

A note on terminology

Much like the terms developers, engineers, and programmers, practitioners in this field also refer to themselves in ways that are mostly the same but mean different things to those who use them.

The two main terms you have likely heard used interchangeably are "technical writing(er)" and "documentation", plus maybe some other terms appended. These terms mean more or less the same thing, at least more so than with programming-related role titles, but many of us still take issue with them and prefer other, more inclusive terms.

For example, as I will cover in *Chapter 8, Collaborative Workflows with Automated Documentation Processes*, a lot of technical explanation is far more than words these days, and our typical titles reflect a rather out-of-date viewpoint. I also believe that a documentation portal may not always be the best place to explain everything. I experimented with "technical communicator" (which I still have on my LinkedIn profile at the time of authoring this book). I've also heard "documentation engineer", which I quite like as it reflects that many of us at smaller companies also build a lot of tooling for documentation. However, what a lot of technical writing communities have settled on to include everyone is "documentarian". It's not perfect, but it reflects that not everyone who contributes to or cares about good documentation has a full-time role dedicated to that task. I assume, much like many of the readers of this book. So, that is the term I will use to refer to you and us throughout the book. Concerning our work, I will use the most relevant term to suit the use case and output. For example, documentation, blog posts, videos, and so on.

I will also use the terms "project" and "product" somewhat interchangeably to refer to what you are documenting. In my mind, a "product" is something commercial, whereas a "project" might not be. However, a few caveats and small differences aside that I will address when I get to them; they are essentially the same.

State of the industry

At the time of writing, the tech industry generally finds itself in an interesting place. The years of wild spending and tech startup valuations are behind us. The unstoppable growth of tech has slowed, and the industry can no longer do whatever it wants and expect no one to question it or everyone to accept it.

No matter what happens in the rest of the tech industry around us, one statistic glaringly remains in survey after survey of developer opinions and ecosystems. People want and need better documentation. The race to build over the past few years led to a plethora of applications that may or may not be well built, but often don't make a lot of sense to internal or external users. There are budget cuts in the industry at the moment, and sometimes, roles outside of engineering are some of the first to go. But if you are open to learning and learning how to learn, there will be a role for you for a while.

It would be naive and dishonest of me to tell you that the industry isn't in the midst of a massive state of change. The last chapters of this book will cover AI-based tools that have swept through everything in the past year or so. It remains to be seen if they are the game changer everyone promises or just another ride of the hype rollercoaster, but there's no doubt that they will affect how we create and consume documentation in the medium term.

Automated tools for generating some parts of documentation have existed for a while, but the new wave of AI-powered options is definitely more powerful and nuanced than anything before. They can't cover the complete documentation requirements yet, but they can fill many gaps and needs. With regards to the state of the industry and our role in it, even if everyone decides to replace their documentation platforms with AI-powered bots, they still need someone to write the source material that feeds the AI for a while. We may write less for direct human consumption, but we will still be writing.

Who this book is for

This book is aimed at those who primarily code, be they developers, support or sales engineers, or existing technically minded technical writers. It's full of advice, tips, and tools to make documentation the best possible with minimal work.

If you're reading this book, you are someone who cares about explaining complex topics in the most effective ways. You may already be an experienced documentarian looking for new ideas and a knowledge top-up. Or maybe you're less experienced but want to do something to improve the current state of a project you contribute to. Whatever your motivation, there will be something for you.

I intend to take you on a journey from teaching you the essentials you need to know to exploring cutting-edge ideas and practice to raise what you create head and shoulders above other projects and products.

What this book covers

Chapter 1, The Why, Who, and How of Technical Writing, talks about all the different stakeholders with an interest in good documentation and what it can accomplish for them.

Chapter 2, Understanding Different Types of Documentation in Software Development, explores the different documentation types that can form documentation.

Chapter 3, Language and the Fundamental Mechanics of Explaining, covers the grammar fundamentals that make documentation clearer and more confident.

Chapter 4, Page Structure and How It Aids Reading, explains how page structure makes content easier for readers.

Chapter 5, The Technical Writing Process, advises on the ideal process to follow for collaborative technical writing.

Chapter 6, Selecting the Right Tools for Efficient Documentation Creation, discusses the options and how to pick the tools to help create, collaborate, and provide documentation to readers.

Chapter 7, Handling Other Content Types for Comprehensive Documentation, explores other types of media to add to documentation that complement your words.

Chapter 8, Collaborative Workflows with Automated Documentation Processes, delves into how you can automate many common processes in creating documentation.

Chapter 9, The Opportunities to Enhance Documentation with AI Tools, talks about how the new wave of AI tools can assist and enhance documentation creation.

Conventions used

There are a number of text conventions used throughout this book.

`Code in text`: Indicates code words in text, database table names, folder names, filenames, file extensions, pathnames, dummy URLs, user input, and Twitter handles. Here is an example: " For AsyncAPI, you use `user` and `signedup`."

A block of code is set as follows:

```
var schema = buildSchema(`
  type Query {
    hello: String
  }
`)
```

> **Tips or important notes**
> Appear like this.

Get in touch

Feedback from our readers is always welcome.

General feedback: If you have questions about any aspect of this book, email us at `customercare@packtpub.com` and mention the book title in the subject of your message.

Errata: Although we have taken every care to ensure the accuracy of our content, mistakes do happen. If you have found a mistake in this book, we would be grateful if you would report this to us. Please visit `www.packtpub.com/support/errata` and fill in the form.

Piracy: If you come across any illegal copies of our works in any form on the internet, we would be grateful if you would provide us with the location address or website name. Please contact us at `copyright@packtpub.com` with a link to the material.

If you are interested in becoming an author: If there is a topic that you have expertise in and you are interested in either writing or contributing to a book, please visit `authors.packtpub.com`.

Share Your Thoughts

Once you've read *Technical Writing for Software Developers*, we'd love to hear your thoughts! Scan the QR code below to go straight to the Amazon review page for this book and share your feedback.

https://packt.link/r/1835080405

Your review is important to us and the tech community and will help us make sure we're delivering excellent quality content.

Download a free PDF copy of this book

Thanks for purchasing this book!

Do you like to read on the go but are unable to carry your print books everywhere?

Is your e-book purchase not compatible with the device of your choice?

Don't worry!, Now with every Packt book, you get a DRM-free PDF version of that book at no cost.

Read anywhere, any place, on any device. Search, copy, and paste code from your favorite technical books directly into your application.

The perks don't stop there, you can get exclusive access to discounts, newsletters, and great free content in your inbox daily

Follow these simple steps to get the benefits:

1. Scan the QR code or visit the following link:

https://packt.link/free-ebook/9781835080405

2. Submit your proof of purchase.
3. That's it! We'll send your free PDF and other benefits to your email directly.

1

The Why, Who, and How of Tech Writing

Tech writing is fundamentally about helping people understand concepts that are potentially complex or new to them. To do this effectively, before you start putting fingers to keys, you need to start by asking three key questions about your subject and the audience(s) for it. After doing this, later and more in-depth parts of the process will become clearer and easier. There are more audiences for your words than you might think, and different audiences have different expectations and needs from documentation. Understanding these will save you hours of work and countless frustrations later. Finally, to help you through those frustrating times, I hope to help you understand how important good tech writing is and what a crucial role you play, whatever the nature of your work is.

This chapter covers the following main topics:

- Why tech writing is important
- What documentarians can accomplish
- How to understand who you are writing for

Why should you care about tech writing?

What's one of the first things you look at when evaluating a new project or service? If the documentation isn't the first thing you look at, I bet it's in the top three. The primary function of documentation is to tell people how to use something, but it also has several crucial secondary purposes that provide value across a company or project team.

To quote a phrase I've used for a while in presentations:

"Documentation isn't just for developers."

Documentation gives confidence in a product making it useful for marketing sales enablement, customer support, **search engine optimization** (**SEO**), and, as we now realize, for myriad other machine-driven purposes.

This section reinforced what you probably already know and feel. After all, you're reading this book! But how can you convince others of the worth of good documentation?

What can documentarians accomplish?

Tech writing often sits between and crosses over multiple teams in a company or project. This means that you have the potential to impact the work and goals of many, even if it's not in your initial job description. This section covers some of the most common teams and departments you might encounter.

Marketing

If a project's documentation is open to the public (not behind a login), it likely fuels a high percentage of searchable text on a website. High-quality, well-written documentation optimized for SEO is a goldmine for search engine traffic. No one wants to read documentation stuffed full of marketing content and working closely with a marketing team to ensure style consistency and break down content silos is essential.

Depending on the size and structure of your company or team, documentarians and marketing teams can work closely together to help this process. You can collaborate on style guides, write technical blog posts, review or edit white papers, and so on.

Product

I'm sure many of you know that good documentation can't hide or improve a bad product. However, for the most part, products and documentation are somewhere between fantastic and terrible. Good documentation brings confidence in a product to a potential customer or user. Later chapters in this book will describe how to make your writing more confident, and this is one of the justifications for that style of writing. Often, someone decides between product options by reading their documentation. The products that sound confident and can do what their documentation promises are likely to appeal more to potential users.

Sales

Sales and sales engineers often have some of their own playbooks and content for working with current and future customers. However, much like with marketing teams, documentarians can work closely with them to ensure materials are consistent and break down those omnipresent content silos.

Support

Customer success, support, or whatever a company calls the team of people who help users achieve their goals are often any documentation team's biggest allies and sources of knowledge. They see how people try to use a product daily. They know where users struggle, what they find confusing, and the common pitfalls they face. These teams also likely maintain their own sources of information or documentation. Again, try to work with them to reduce these silos, but regularly syncing with them gives you a great source of information for what documentation is missing and how effective current documentation is.

Developer relations

Though they are often part of sales or marketing teams, developer relations teams are typically out speaking with developers, convincing them, and helping them use a product. The content they produce could be one of the first things that a potential user sees, so again, work with them to ensure consistency of message, reduce silos, and much like support, find out what they feel is missing from the documentation that would help users.

Engineering

Fundamentally, documentation exists to make what product teams created understandable. Or, as I like to say:

"Documentation makes engineering look good."

If you're reading this book, then you're probably an engineer. So, I phrase this section slightly differently from the other teams' sections. Documentarians need to get details from engineering to explain how a product works and how to use it. There is frequently a disconnect between what engineering thinks is important, what documentarians think is important, and what users think is important. I dig deeper into this topic throughout the book, but briefly, cast aside your assumptions and in-depth knowledge and think about how someone completely new perceives what you have built.

Machine readers

It may or may not surprise you that much of the traffic to your documentation probably doesn't come from human readers. Website scrapers, sitemap builders, and a variety of other machines trawl your documentation regularly. While documentarians are typically aware of SEO, the implementation of best practices can vary. This is another perfect opportunity to work with marketing teams to improve the visibility of documentation and surface it to potential customers even more than it already is.

However, SEO and "traditional" crawlers are old news. The new machines trawling your documentation in great numbers are feeding training data for **large language models** (**LLMs**) (`https://en.wikipedia.org/wiki/Large_language_model`). Whether you like this or not, if your documentation is public and for a moderately high-profile product, then until we agree on a standard way to block this happening, it's probably already too late. I cover the rapidly changing topic of **artificial intelligence** (**AI**) and documentation in greater detail later, but right now, be aware that an increasing amount of people are interacting with the words you write in myriad ways.

Proofreading for accuracy and safety

Unless my memory fails me, I have never worked documenting any "mission-critical" product. There were undoubtedly products that were very important to customers, and any downtime or poor information would impact their business. But typically, any product issues are covered by **service-level agreements** (**SLAs**) (`https://en.wikipedia.org/wiki/Service-level_agreement`), which don't often cover documentation issues.

For the most part, if someone finds an error or inaccuracy, I can almost immediately fix it and roll out a new version. While that inaccuracy might have caused inconvenience, it's unlikely to have caused a major loss of money, time, or life. Thankfully. However, I have met many documentarians working on projects and with toolchains that don't allow this luxury or flexibility. I once met someone who created the documentation for rolling out Google's data centers. They had to print all documentation as there was no internet access allowed, and if someone found an error, they had to print new copies. Any error – for example, an instruction to plug a cable into the wrong socket – could cost millions in revenue per day. I also met documentarians who work for Schindler. Again, their installation engineers receive hard copies of documentation, and installing an elevator or escalator incorrectly costs money and can cost lives.

Content silos

I mentioned content silos several times in previous sections. I have never worked at a company where these didn't exist but keeping them in check is important. Regarding documentation and documentarians, the content other teams create is an excellent source of what's missing from the documentation. I appreciate that documentation teams are often far outnumbered by other teams, and this is what causes these teams to create what they need in the first place. One of the aims of this chapter is to help you justify your role and, hopefully, grow its capacity. The fact that other teams are creating content that they feel is missing can be an effective justification for increasing documentarian capacity. It's not the only reason other teams create what you can consider documentation (companies are full of politics, after all), but it's one potential reason.

Writer in the middle

In summary, as you can hopefully see, documentarians and their work sit in the middle of many different roles and teams. This position comes with positives and negatives that are worth knowing. Even if you don't intend to move into a full-time documentation role, it's worth knowing what they could be, as, at the very least, it will help you empathize with those who are.

Even if you are one of the most level-headed people, gathering, processing, and acting on all these potential inputs is overwhelming. A documentarian can be such a fountain of knowledge, knowing a small to medium amount about numerous topics, that it can become frustrating to know what to do with all this knowledge. You might feel motivated to get involved in too many activities or try to fix too many things. Again, attempting this is overwhelming and, depending on your company, unwelcome. One of the biggest frustrations I have personally found as a long-term documentarian is that you often hear internally and externally that documentation is important. Reading this book, you probably already know and agree with this. However, the reality of the documentarian role is that you often don't feel as important as everyone says you are. Some of this comes from expectations versus assumptions. Almost everyone has an opinion on when documentation is "wrong," but fewer can tell you what they would do about it or when it is "right." Documentation is front and center in nearly every product but is often created and crafted behind the scenes by people who like to think in the written word and don't always speak up. Documentarians lack the kudos and credibility of programmers and engineers. They are often not in a position to push product ideas forward, yet they can tie all of these teams together.

Switching to the positives, while gathering and processing so much information can be overwhelming, it is also rewarding. Documentarians are often the first testers of a new product or feature, the first to find issues, and the first to follow a user workflow outside of a development team. If you enjoy exploring or figuring things out, creating documentation is an ideal role for you. You are often provided with a sketch or a draft of a product or feature and need to figure out in more detail how it works and how to explain it to an audience. In software documentation, this involves understanding a broad range of programming languages, frameworks, and techniques and learning how a user is likely to use those in a real-world scenario.

The most significant positive is knowing that, even though you may not always hear from them directly, your words will impact people as they try to accomplish their goals.

Understanding who you are writing for

You're in front of the keyboard, and an editor opens with a blinking cursor. You have a brief and have experimented with a prototype. Now comes the task of figuring out how to explain that prototype to different user groups and profiles.

While reducing a discussion to an acronym may sound like a cliché, I typically start by thinking of the three *Ws*:

- *Who* is reading a document?

- *What* do they want to accomplish?

- *Why* do they want to accomplish it?

Even if you haven't addressed these Ws, other members of your company likely have, and you can leverage their work in yours.

Your product, project, or feature possibly has multiple user profiles, and the type of documentation you need to produce can vary for each one. Functional user profiles are easier to break down and analyze, as someone whose job involves task A is more likely interested in documents that describe how to undertake task A rather than B. The level of complexity and the content are more subtle than this, and you can make some general assumptions based on the type of document someone is reading (I will dig more into what these different document types can be later).

Someone reading API or reference documentation probably has an idea of something specific they want to understand and know the functional facts. Someone reading a quick start is probably newer to a project and would like an opinionated introduction. Reference documentation and a quick start guide are two reasonably clear ends of the documentation spectrum. In between is the tricky part and the part where you will spend the most time.

If you are documenting a simpler project or a project with a focused use case, then this task is easier than something more broad and general purpose.

I appreciate that, as with many technical topics, everything depends, and implementation relates to the use case. It's usually easier to follow with an example that walks through a thought process instead of talking in abstractions. So, let's move on to a practical example.

Learning by example

For example, a geocoding library has far fewer functions and applications than a database or a programming language. Guessing what someone might want to do with any general-purpose tool is challenging and will take a while to perfect. Let's take an example project used throughout the book. I assume that you are working on a greenfield project, but many of the same principles apply if you work on a pre-existing project.

Monito is a tool for monitoring application performance and errors. Monito comes in two versions: a self-hosted version where you have to connect it to your own backend and analysis tools to gather, save, and analyze data, and a hosted version that plugs right into a data store and dashboard service.

My recommendation is to start with the beginning and end of the journey and slowly fill in the gaps over time. Monito has two starter paths. There's only one of you documenting the project, and time is tight. So, which should you document? *Chapter 5* covers the full documentation process. For now, you get a strong indication that as much as the project wants to support everyone's choice of integration tools, documenting all those possibilities will take too much time right now. So, you decide to start with documenting the hosted version.

To get started with the hosted version, a user must choose a **software development kit** (**SDK**) in their application code. Again, Monito offers SDKs for many languages. User research shows that the most popular are **JavaScript**, **Python**, and **Go**. So for now, you decide only to show examples for those but mention that other options are available.

The user then needs to register an account for an SDK key that identifies them as the user and instantiate the SDK with that key, so you show how to do that with the three chosen SDKs.

Next, you show how to trigger key events using the SDK in the three languages and how they appear in the hosted dashboard.

Finally, you summarize what the guide covered and point people to the next steps.

That covers the quick start. What about the reference documentation? For now, as a lot of interaction with the service is via SDKs and the development team has stuck to well-established best practices while building the SDKs, you decide to stick with autogenerated documentation from the SDKs. This is enough for those who want to dig into what else is possible after following the quick start.

A week or two after release, you start receiving user feedback. More users want to know how to self-host than expected, and many users want to integrate Monito with a popular alerting tool to know when it detects important errors. So, you need to document these two guides and any supporting material around them for your next priorities. The product team also tells you that they're shipping a new feature soon that allows users to define custom data structures to send to Monito, and that also needs documenting and adding to the quick start.

Thus, the process is ongoing. You slowly fill in missing documentation gaps based on user requirements, product requirements, and feedback.

Don't forget the end users and the end-end users

I have spent most of my career working on documentation for developer tools. So, this book's focus is more geared toward tools others use to build products for end users. This means there's an extra level of interpretation above the documentation I create that the reader interprets into another application or code base that might even have its own documentation. I like to call these users "end-end users." While it's difficult to guess what that end-end use case might be, if you can find out via support channels, it can help you narrow down use cases and user journeys when you want some semblance of focus.

Take the Monito example. Currently, the documentation covers general use cases for those incorporating the tool into their own tools. Through user research, you find that Monito has a large user base in the finance sector. This gives you a slightly clearer idea about examples you can use in code snippets and explanations.

Summary

This chapter covered some fundamental building blocks of technical writing and creating documentation. It looked at why technical writing and documentation are important and what stakeholders often look for and expect with documentation.

You learned how to identify intended users reading documentation and what they want to understand and accomplish.

Finally, this chapter aimed to inspire you to keep at it when dealing with and balancing all the different stakeholders, users, and their needs.

The next chapter looks at the different types of documentation you might need to create and the purpose of each type.

2

Understanding Different Types of Documentation in Software Development

Chapter 1 of this book looked at why you and your project or product should even care about documentation. With the convincing and scene setting complete, it's time to start looking at the mechanics of good documentation, starting with the types of documentation you might need to create.

The simplest documentation can be a single README file in a code repository, while the most complex could be a series of interconnected sections, topics, and sub-projects. As documentation expands into more complex territory, it's likely to need different sorts of pages that cover different purposes and have different structures. This chapter covers the common section types you might typically have in most documentation, what they are likely to contain, and the templates you can use to create them.

Different people have different names for these sections, but the content in each section is loosely the same and fall into the following categories:

- Getting started, onboarding, or QuickStart
- Tutorials, guides, or how-tos
- Reference
- Blogs

So, let's get started!

Templates

Before getting started, I want to provide a quick diversion that covers templates and how to apply and use them before you start documentation from scratch. Content templates typically consist of headings or sections that you can add to different content types, optionally with prompts and guidance on what to add under each heading. Over time, documentarians tend to create their own templates, adding them to content creation workflows for all to use. If you're unsure where to start with templates, I recommend community resources such as the Good Docs project (`https://thegooddocsproject.dev`), which has worked hard to create many starter documentation templates for people to pick up and use. For each content type covered in this chapter, I include links to relevant templates from the project and/or my thoughts on a template you can start with.

So, let's actually get started.

Getting started and onboarding

This content type helps people learn how to get started with a project or features.

Most inexperienced users start their journey with you via a *Getting Started* guide or onboarding experience. Getting Started, sometimes called a QuickStart, is typically a text-based guide that contains other media or interactive components.

Onboarding is sometimes called a tour or in-app help and is typically part of an app or product experience. It contains text that you might be involved in creating (I would say "should," but that's not always the case).

A detailed overview of Getting Started

I already covered some aspects of creating Getting Started guides in *Chapter 1*, but it's a big topic, so the content you are likely to spend the most initial time on is worth covering in more detail. Whether you call it Getting Started, QuickStart, or onboarding, the first steps a user or potential user makes with a product are crucial.

Onboarding is slightly different as it's likely that a user has already created an account, but in some respects, you have more to prove, even if people are taking advantage of a free trial, as they have given personal information to you. Typically, you have little identity, tracking, or metrics information on someone reading documentation.

Documentarians are a key part of **developer experience** (**DX**), a growing movement of practices and professionals that focus on making developers' technical lives as frictionless as possible.

There is a popular metric in DX called *time to first hello world* or *time to Getting Started*. While a *Hello World* example is a time-honored tradition for introducing readers to a technical product, it's not always relevant or a particularly good way of showcasing a product. Whether or not you use an example that shows a "hello world" message, the term has become a common term for showing someone the basic steps for using a technical product.

And why is time important? There are a lot of potential competitors for business and attention, and wasting people's time following a Getting Started guide that doesn't work, is too complex, doesn't show anything useful, is poorly written, or has a multitude of other problems detract from highlighting what you've built. I provide more detail on how to avoid these potential issues generally in documentation throughout this book, particularly in *Chapter 3* (for improving language), *Chapter 4* (for improving structure), *Chapter 7* (for improving code examples), and *Chapter 8* (for testing code examples). You should pay extra attention to all these in a Getting Started guide. While all your documentation will leave a lasting impression on readers, if a Getting Started guide doesn't deliver, you won't have a chance to leave that impression.

But how do you decide what to include in a Getting Started guide?

You need to show what makes your project special. What makes it special among anything similar? And yes, despite how unique you might think what you've built is, there are always other options in the eyes of a potential user. Often, the most common alternative is "do it myself." What makes you the best option might not always be obvious. Maybe you are faster, more secure, use fewer dependencies, or are cheaper. These are all perfectly good points of differentiation to highlight and can be enough to make someone choose your product over another.

Learning with an example

The example project in this book, Monito, exists in a busy ecosystem with many other alerting and observability tools. Here are some features that you can mention to make Monito stand out in a Getting Started guide:

- It's available as a hosted or self-hosted option

- You can use it with many different programming languages

- The dashboard allows non-developers to analyze and prioritize errors

It's impossible to cover all of these in detail in the Getting Started guide, but you can mention them when relevant and provide convenient jumping-off points to those wanting to learn more. I covered what I thought should be in the Monito Getting Started guide in *Chapter 1*, but this explains some of my thought processes as to why I included what I did, in addition to the basic and necessary steps, such as creating an account, installing dependencies, and so on. To reiterate, here are the two most important things a Getting Started guide should do:

- It should highlight what makes your product great and why someone should use it

- The guide should follow an opinionated path that showcases the first point but can offer links to where to find alternative paths and more information

That should have given you a lot to think about. So, what templates can help with this work?

Templates for a Getting Started guide

Ideally, a Getting Started guide should have content under the following headings:

- **Overview**: What the reader can expect from the guide.

- **Prerequisites**: What steps the reader needs to take before starting the guide.

- **Installation**: How to install any components that are needed.

- **Setup**: How to set up the components that are needed.

- **Parts**: A series of tasks that form the guide. These are individual headings that should actively describe what the reader will learn and accomplish:

  - **Steps**: Each step is under the task. These are individual headings that should actively describe what the reader will learn and accomplish.

- **Summary**: What did the reader learn in this guide, and why is it useful and relevant?

- **Next steps**: Where to go next to build upon the knowledge learned.

> **Further reading**
>
> Refer to the Good Docs project's QuickStart template for more details and ideas: `https://gitlab.com/tgdp/templates/-/blob/main/quickstart/template-quickstart.md`.

Once you've introduced a reader to your project, the next steps are to help them learn more about the features and use cases that are relevant to them.

Tutorials

If a Getting Started guide showcases what's best about your product and gets new users started on their journey with you, then tutorials, sometimes called how-tos or guides, take them on the next steps.

As you might expect, the breadth and detail of tutorials or guides depends on your project, but here's my general advice.

If your product or project has identifiable sections or sub-projects, they need tutorial sections. Do you support different ways to use your product – for example, a **Command-Line Integration (CLI)** tool, a visual interface, and an **Application Programming Interface (API)**? Perhaps you also support **continuous integration (CI)** or have applications and plugins in third-party marketplaces? If so, all of these need at least one tutorial on how to use them. If one of these sub-areas is particularly complex – for example, the visual interface has many different sections, or the **Software development kit (SDK)** consists of several components – then again, each needs at least one tutorial.

There has been a lot of discussion among documentarians about whether it's better to organize tutorials and guides by function or use case – That is, by an internal "what something does" view or an external "what someone wants to do with it" view. If you are building a project for a specific purpose or industry, then you can make more assumptions about what someone might do with your project, but for more general-purpose tools, especially to begin with, it can be hard to make these assumptions until later.

I recommend starting with sections on "what something does," as that is easier for you to know where and how to start. Then, over time, you can add the "what someone wants to do with it" as you learn from users and their requests, possibly even replacing the other content. There is some overlap between this style of content and reference documentation. In my opinion, most reference documentation is functional and probably even autogenerated, whereas functional tutorials add more of a human touch, describing the steps and usage of those components concerning others. One thing to note is that people often ask for more "use case-focused" content without knowing what they mean. Or they are looking for something specific to them that they assume applies to other users or are looking for something that answers all their nuanced questions. Pragmatically speaking, we know that accomplishing those requirements for everyone is almost impossible, which is why, despite our best efforts, most people are never entirely satisfied with documentation, as it can't answer everyone's precise questions and use cases. That's not to say you shouldn't try to meet and exceed people's expectations – my point is more that you need time to do so.

Expanding on the example

Let's continue with the Monito example. The Getting Started guide took users on an opinionated path and highlighted some of Monito's key features. What do you give more detail on? *Chapter 1* mentioned two potential tutorials, one on self-hosting and one on connecting an alerting tool. That's two good starting points. You can also create versions of the QuickStart that cover the "less popular" programming language options and the QuickStart mentioned "next step" features, so those also need tutorials. There's already an emerging potential structure for the tutorials. From a functional structural perspective, this could be as follows:

- QuickStart
- SDKs:
  - Python
  - Go
  - JavaScript
  - Ruby
  - C++

- Features:
  - Hosted dashboard
  - Advanced alerting
  - Conditional alerting
  - Creating custom metadata
- iSelf-hosting:
  - Docker
  - Kubernetes
  - Bare metal
- Integrations:
  - Alerting tools
  - Alternative backends
- Exporting data

Templates for tutorials

While the exact headings that form a tutorial vary based on the topic, here are some suggestions for common ones:

- **Overview**: What the reader can expect from the guide.
- **Prerequisites**: The steps the reader must take before starting the guide.
- **Parts**: A series of tasks that form the guide. These are individual headings that should describe actively what the reader will learn and accomplish:
  - **Steps**: Each step under the task. These are individual headings that should describe actively what the reader will learn and accomplish.
- **Summary**: What the reader learned in this guide, and why is it useful and relevant?
- **Next steps**: Where to go next to build upon the knowledge learned.

> **Further reading**
>
> For more details and ideas, refer to the Good Docs project's how-to template (`https://gitlab.com/tgdp/templates/-/blob/main/quickstart/template-quickstart.md`) and tutorial template (`https://gitlab.com/tgdp/templates/-/blob/main/tutorial/template-tutorial.md`).

Before leaving the topic of tutorials, there is one slightly different tutorial worth paying extra attention to: tutorials for using an **API**.

API onboarding tutorials

Most API documentation is in the form of reference documentation, something covered in more detail later in this chapter. How much more you need to cover APIs in tutorials depends on the complexity of your APIs and how fundamental they are to the product.

If your product uses a relatively simple or standard API pattern and is one similar interaction option among many, you probably don't need many tutorials in addition to the reference documentation. It's probably worth mentioning that it's also possible to accomplish the tasks you cover in tutorials with an API and where to go for more details.

If your API is the core way that users interact with your product, then fill your tutorials with further references on using and assembling API components. You should also still include the API reference documentation, as that's how some would rather consume information, and you can likely autogenerate it.

If your API is complex or non-standard, you need tutorials to help people understand how to use it. As someone close to the project, you may not know if it's complex or non-standard and probably think it isn't. *Chapters 3* and *4* cover some ways to reframe your thinking about what you work on, but in summary, if you're not following API standards, then it's non-standard and maybe complex.

In my experience, often, one of the more confusing parts of using an API is the initial and ongoing authentication. Despite several standard methods for doing so, almost every API I ever use does something slightly different, and frequently, it makes it irritatingly hard to figure out what you're supposed to do. Details on how to authenticate (and remain authenticated) can be a part of the reference or tutorial documentation, but make sure it's somewhere clear and that wherever else it's relevant as a prerequisite, it's also clear.

Reference

This section includes technical details of how individual components, functions, or APIs work.

I have always considered the differentiation between reference documentation and everything else in the following way:

- A reference document tells you that a hammer is for hitting things, wood is from dead trees that you can build things with, and nails are small, sharp, pointed bits of metal

- A guide or tutorial tells you how to build a shed with wood, hammer, and nails

Depending on the project and technology type, a reference section could include the following:

- SDK function details

- API endpoint details

- Architecture and design details

- Security and privacy details

- Whitepapers and academic papers

The terms API and SDK can sometimes be used interchangeably, depending on the project or product.

I start with SDK documentation, as you can typically build the reference documentation as you build your code.

Most SDK methods help end users perform certain functions with your underlying applications, with optional input or output parameters and variables. Methods are typically building blocks of applications, so you only need to explain how each building block works.

As a developer who cares about documentation, I assume you're already adding code comments. If not, add that to the to-do list. It helps a lot with documentation in general as it forces you to think about how to explain what the different parts of your code do.

Almost all programming languages support built-in or popular third-party tools for generating reference documentation from code comments.

With some languages and tools, you must use certain syntax or add annotations to code comments to mark out input and output parameters, while others detect this automatically.

If there are important connections and interactions between methods, then mention those in the comments, and typically, if you follow certain language-specific standards, these links remain when rendering the documentation.

For example, you can use JSDoc (`https://jsdoc.app/about-getting-started`) for JavaScript comments:

```
/**
 * Represents a book.
 * @constructor
```

```
 * @param {string} title - The title of the book.
 * @param {string} author - The author of the book.
 * @return {string} book - The full book title
 */
function Book(title, author) {
    return title + ", " + author
}
```

The preceding code uses the `param` and `return` tags above the method, followed by the type to indicate the input and output parameters, and renders the rest of the text around these for further context. It has many other blocks and inline (inside the method) tags for other purposes, such as `link` to reference other methods.

The Rust language is well known for its focus on documentation practices and has a comprehensive code documentation tool built into the toolchain (`https://doc.rust-lang.org/rustdoc/how-to-write-documentation.html`). Here's an example of its code comments:

```
//! Fast and easy queue abstraction.
//!
//! Provides an abstraction over a queue.  When the abstraction is
used
//! there are these advantages:
//! - Fast
//! - [`Easy`]
//!
//! [`Easy`]: http://thatwaseasy.example.com

/// This module makes it easy.
pub mod easy {

    /// Use the abstraction function to do this specific thing.
    pub fn abstraction() {}

}
```

Adding good code comments adds more than being rendered as static documentation on a web page. Different tools make use of code comments to render help text. For example, your IDE often shows them when you hover your mouse over method names and variables. Package pages, such as details on the node package manager or PyPi, often show elements of code comments rendered on web pages or installer tools. New AI tools use these code comments to make judgments, assumptions, and patterns about code from questions. In summary, good code documentation helps many people in multiple contexts, so it's worth considering adding it to the best of your ability as you craft code.

In addition to code, one of the most common sections of reference documentation is for APIs.

API documentation

Next, I cover API documentation, as it's one of the options with many existing well-defined standards, specifications, and toolchains.

Like SDK methods, API endpoints generally consist of inputs with parameters and outputs with return values. APIs are the building blocks behind applications, ferrying requests and responses between application components and applications spread around the internet. Therefore, you can also create API reference documentation that describes the building blocks and explains how those building blocks fit together with other areas of documentation.

There are two main ways to autogenerate API reference documentation. One is from the code methods, which, depending on the programming language you use and the structure of your applications, might be the same methods that form part of the SDK or different ones. Some languages use special annotations in method comments to denote that they are used for API endpoints, and you can generate documentation using the same tools and methods as when generating SDK documentation.

However, one of the more common approaches is to generate documentation from an API specification. To confuse matters even more, these specifications could be written before writing any code, and you can generate stub code from the specification or vice versa. It mostly depends on who designs and collaborates on the API design and if they prefer working in code or spec files. Whichever method you choose, thankfully, as there are API specification standards, you end up with the same set of properties and parameters, so from a documentation perspective, there are not many changes in what or how to document, just where.

For the most part, when people think of API specifications, they think of OpenAPI (`https://www.openapis.org`) (previously known as Swagger), and from the "old days" of API specs, it's pretty much only OpenAPI and RAML (`https://raml.org`) that still survive as far as I know. Technically speaking, these are **Representational State Transfer** APIs, better known to many as **REST** or HTTP APIs, as they follow the design patterns of HTTP methods for accessing resources on the internet. However, the world of API specs has grown in different directions, and depending on the ecosystem you spend the most time in, you may be more familiar with newer alternatives, such as **GraphQL** (`https://graphql.org/`) or **AsyncAPI** (`https://www.asyncapi.com`).

This book isn't the place to discuss why these alternatives exist or how they work. The most important aspect for documentation is that the alternatives exist because their creators felt that HTTP APIs no longer represented increasingly common application design and architecture methods. This means that the way you document these standards is also different.

When documenting REST/HTTP APIs, you generally focus on input parameters, what the endpoint does with those, and what it returns as an output variable. It's fairly similar to documenting SDK methods, just language-neutral. The OpenAPI spec consists of multiple object types, all with description fields to add instructive text and provide meaningful parameter names and error messages. The following example consists of one users endpoint with a description and a description of the values it returns:

```
openapi: 3.0.0
info:
  title: Sample API
  description: Optional multiline or single-line description in
[CommonMark](http://commonmark.org/help/) or HTML.
  version: 0.1.9
servers:
  - url: http://api.example.com/v1
    description: Optional server description, e.g. Main (production)
server
  - url: http://staging-api.example.com
    description: Optional server description, e.g. Internal staging
server for testing

paths:
  /users:
    get:
      summary: Returns a list of users.
      description: Optional extended description in CommonMark or
HTML.
      responses:
        '200':    # status code
          description: A JSON array of user names
          content:
            application/json:
              schema:
                type: array
                items:
                  type: string
```

Documentation tools take this spec and render it in a more readable way, using the descriptions to provide context and present the input and output parameter information:

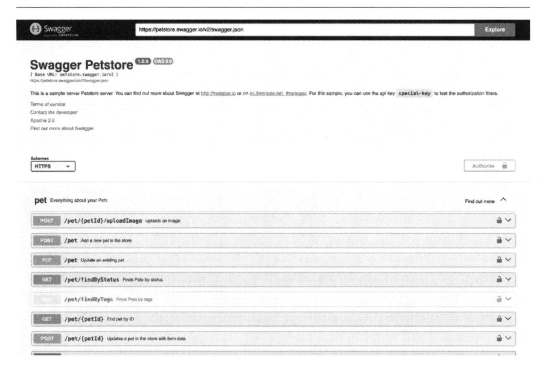

Figure 2.4 – The layout of the Swagger UI rendered API specification

GraphQL

GraphQL looks at querying data in quite different ways, which can initially be confusing. Instead of presenting a series of endpoints, it defines a series of types and functions you query. From a documentation perspective, it promised to make APIs "self-documenting." It may not surprise you to hear that this isn't strictly true. It's more than that, though – GraphQL organizes around data structures, queries, and methods. To someone who knows what they're looking at, it's more explainable. There is a specification for GraphQL APIs, but generally, you define it directly in code. The following example (taken from graphql.org) is a standard "hello world" example, but it's defined as a spec and JavaScript code that executes that spec:

```
var { graphql, buildSchema } = require("graphql")

// Construct a schema, using GraphQL schema language
var schema = buildSchema(`
  type Query {
    hello: String
  }
`)
```

```
// The rootValue provides a resolver function for each API endpoint
var rootValue = {
  hello: () => {
    return "Hello world!"
  },
}

// Run the GraphQL query '{ hello }' and print out the response
graphql({
  schema,
  source: "{ hello }",
  rootValue,
}).then(response => {
  console.log(response)
})
```

As the assumption is that GraphQL is "self-explanatory" for developers, a GraphQL endpoint typically offers an interactive "explorer" where developers can explore how to use it. There are also documentation tools that render the spec in a more readable way.

However, I have heard from many developers that this is often not enough, so you might want to consider some guides or additional reference content.

AsyncAPI

Traditionally, HTTP and REST APIs are reactive. You send a request and wait for a response. Most modern applications send and receive dozens to hundreds and thousands of requests and responses per second, and while modern language options for using HTTP and REST APIs support asynchronous requests (that is, one request shouldn't block any other process from happening), AsyncAPI is one of many new event-driven tools that react to events generated by applications instead of a series of requests and responses. While the technical implementation differs from HTTP and REST APIs, the API specification isn't too different from OpenAPI. You write in YAML, but instead of paths and operations, you use channels and operations as event-driven architecture is all about "subscribing" to events, and I think subscribing to a channel is a familiar concept to many. This does mean that the verbs you use to describe operations are different. You might use "user" and "signup" for an HTTP and REST API. For AsyncAPI, you would use user and signedup. The following example lists the "operations" to expect requests to and "channels" define the inputs to expect and the outputs to return:

```
asyncapi: 3.0.0g
info:
  title: Cool Example
  version: 0.1.0
channels:
  userSignedUp:
```

```
    address: user/signedup
    messages:
      userSignedUp:
        description: An event describing that a user just signed up.
        payload:
          type: object
          properties:
            fullName:
              type: string
            email:
              type: string
              format: email
            age:
              type: integer
              minimum: 18
operations:
  userSignedUp:
    action: send
    channel:
      $ref: '#/channels/userSignedUp'
```

The "Generator" (https://www.asyncapi.com/tools/generator) is AsyncAPI's official tool for rendering the spec as documentation, but other community tools also exist.

Other standards

Before you start sending feedback, yes, I know there is also **Simple Object Access Protocol** (**SOAP**). The SOAP API is fairly old in technology terms but still popular in risk-averse businesses such as finance or bookings. Some of this is due to not wanting to change something that works, but it's also more secure and gives more implementation options. SOAP focuses on "messages," and you define the API in XML, which you either love or hate depending on your background as a programmer or documentarian. There are a handful of tools for rendering SOAP specs as documentation.

Finally, other inter-application communication protocols exist, such as web sockets and **Google Remote Procedure Call** (**gRPC**). However, these don't have any special documentation steps beyond following standard code documentation practices as they are methods for implementing an API, not an API standard.

Architecture and design details

Less common in reference sections are architecture and internal design details. These are less common because not all projects need them, or smaller teams lack the resources to produce such documentation and point people to code instead. Reference material such as this is useful for projects consisting of complex, interrelated parts with numerous combination possibilities. Good examples are distributed systems with components you can deploy to different locations or something such as Kubernetes, which has multiple required and optional components. Reference documentation of this type shouldn't replace essential onboarding or tutorials – that is, how to fit components together in common use cases – it's more for explaining the theoretical underpinnings of these components.

Security and privacy details

These aren't details about your company or website, such as regional privacy or legal notices, but about your project's internal algorithms or precautions – For example, encryption methods, what is encrypted, when telemetry data is sent to any central servers, and how the project writes data to any databases.

Whitepapers and academic papers

These are one of the least common types of reference documentation but are common in certain projects such as blockchain, other cryptographically-heavy projects, or technically novel projects. These often explain the theory behind the project before any coding was attempted. They are often interesting and inspirational to some users and readers. If you are working on a project that's a canonical standard or protocol for others to implement, then your reference section is crucial, and possibly most of your documentation is of this type.

Templates

Templates for reference sections vary massively, so instead of presenting ideal headings, refer to the following Good Docs project templates for ideas:

- API reference template: `https://gitlab.com/tgdp/templates/-/blob/main/api-reference/template-api-reference.md`

- Concept template: `https://gitlab.com/tgdp/templates/-/blob/main/concept/template-concept.md`

- Reference template: `https://gitlab.com/tgdp/templates/-/blob/main/reference/template-reference.md`

Technical blog posts

A blog post is an end-to-end, self-contained piece of content, normally outside of documentation, that teaches the reader a practical technical lesson.

While not always a content type a documentarian is asked to write, you may be asked to help out, especially in smaller companies where you are one of the few people with the desire and skills to communicate clearly. Blog posts are often a good way to learn about a product or feature from start to finish. As blogs are usually promoted by marketing, outside of QuickStarts, they are also often the first way someone discovers a project, so they are worth doing well.

Much of the advice on structure and language presented in this book for documentation also applies to technical blog posts. There are a couple of main differences.

People generally read documentation when they need to, dipping in and out to find the information they need at the time, whereas most people read a blog post from start to finish, hopefully trying what they learn as they follow. This means that while I promote using consistent examples and a structure that takes people through logical steps in documentation, many documentarians secretly know that that's not how most people consume documentation. With a blog post, you can be more certain, so using a cohesive narrative is more important.

Generally, documentation is quite dry and uses a neutral personality. It's not something covered in this book, but personality and humor are hard to get right, so it's often easier to leave it out. Also, documentation is often an ongoing and collaborative task, so it's easier to use a neutral tone and style that all contributors can align with. However, you can show a little more personality in a blog post. This is still a technical blog post, and for reasons I cover in *Chapter 3*, leaning too far toward overly chatty or light-hearted can cause a reader to lose trust in what you're saying.

I have been explicitly saying "technical blog post" in this section, as often, a "blog post" from technical companies is marketing-heavy, and technically minded people are renowned for – how shall I put it – strongly disliking marketing talk. That's not to say that a technical blog post can't help marketing achieve its goals, but it should do it by showing something awesome or by presenting useful information, not by using overly sales-heavy or unnecessarily positive language.

In summary, present the facts, write well, and add a dash of personality, and you have a great blog post!

Summary

This chapter covered the different documentation types you need to create to fully document a project or product. These are as follows:

- **Getting started, onboarding, or QuickStart**: How people take the first steps with your project or product and some of the standout features
- **Tutorials, guides, or how -tos**: Further step-by-step instructions that cover particular use cases or features
- **Reference**: In-depth details about the function of individual components or the principles behind them

The next chapters cover how to write the content for these document types, starting with every writer's favorite topic… grammar!

3
Language and the Fundamental Mechanics of Explaining

How often have you read documentation to be left uncertain if the recommendations or details you read are what you should follow? It may have contained plenty of technical details and code examples that you thought were relevant to you, but you were left unclear on which to implement and how.

These are likely relevant criticisms of any documentation. As we all know, documentation is hard. What I mean is, did you trust it? Were you confident in what it said? Did you believe what it said was as correct as possible, all caveats aside? *Chapter 2* covered the different types of documentation you might need to produce. This chapter looks at ensuring that all the words you fill that documentation with are clear, confident, and trusted by the people you want to read it.

A lot of people write without confidence, especially in technical documentation. That's OK! There are many reasons people aren't confident when they write, and the next section looks at them in detail.

This chapter covers the following main topics:

- Common reasons for not writing confidently
- How to improve your writing
- Inclusive language

Common reasons for not writing confidently

Some are born with a pen in their hands, their fingers on the keyboard, and words flow from their brains easily. Well, they appear to anyway. But for many of us, writing can be a slow process, and different reasons cause our writing not to be the best it could be. This section looks at some of the most common and how to improve them.

Not a native speaker

Let's face it. While a lot of documentation is in English, many of its readers and writers don't have English as their native language. English is wonderfully vague and flexible, which is one reason it remains popular and successful as a global language of communication. However, it is full of strange subtleties, and while many understand it, few understand it to an advanced level. This includes many of those who have it as a native language. Many of us learn very little about its grammar and advanced usage. I had my last formal English grammar lesson when I was about 15. English has multiple *flavours*. I used the non-American spelling there on purpose as I am primarily a British and Australian English speaker, forced to use American English most of the time, weeping all the time while simultaneously realizing that few would even be speaking English if it weren't for America… I digress. What I mean is that even within "English," there are differences and subtleties that make no sense to its own speakers.

George Bernard Shaw once said, "*England and America are two countries separated by the same language.*"

It took me moving to a country that spoke a different language (Germany) to start re-analyzing and learning my language. This coincided with my use and involvement with the **Vale** language **linter** (more on that in *Chapters 6* and *9*), which meant I needed to start breaking grammatical rules down and thus understand them much more.

Anyway, this chapter intends not to be a dry grammar lesson but to teach you a handful of tips and tricks to lift your grammar use and increase confidence in your writing. However, I am still covering grammar, so while I try not to give you nightmares of school lessons, I might occasionally. It's worth it – I promise!

Intentionally vague

Why would you want to make writing intentionally lacking confidence, unclear, or vague? There are reasons. I won't say "valid reasons" as I don't think they are valid, but there you go. One is a lack of knowledge, which relates to my earlier point. Often, when people write English without understanding its best practices, they tend to stuff their writing with unnecessary words to compensate or sometimes to show off. I don't mean this as a negative criticism. Understandably, someone would think clever words equal clever writing, but it's not true. And remember that I said many documentation consumers aren't reading in their native language? Well, stuffing text with unnecessary words also makes it harder for them to read and understand.

Returning to showing off, I am sorry to say, developers, but often you also tend to want to use documentation to show how clever your coding skills are. I get it! I understand! I cover how to demonstrate your programming prowess better later.

Marketing and product reasons

This reason is possibly the hardest for writers and developers to counter. Documentation isn't the place for marketing messaging, but often, as it's one of the most popular destinations on a website, it's used for that purpose. Documentation should deal with cold, hard facts. Marketing – well, let's be honest – doesn't always. This isn't a book about marketing writing – quite the opposite – but try your best to keep marketing-style language out of documentation. Let the documentation and the quality of the product sell itself, not unclear writing. The same applies to product decisions. Often, a product team wants documentation to hide problems or inadequacies through intentionally vague language or offer promises that may or may not be true. Again, try your best to push back on this. Honest, believable documentation sells a product far more.

Reducing cognitive load

Another common thread that runs through most of the advice here is about reducing the cognitive load on readers as they try to understand complex concepts. Everything you can do to reduce that is a positive. They will probably figure out what you mean by rereading and trial and error, so initially, these small issues don't seem like such a big deal. But multiply them by all the small issues, and they add up, increasing the confusion and frustration a user experiences trying to understand your documentation.

Inclusive language

While it doesn't directly affect the understandability of documentation, using inclusive and accessible language broadens the potential audience and improves readability. In my opinion, non-inclusive language is a language that is the following:

- Patronizing
- Rude
- Overly negative
- Biased
- Outdated
- Unhelpful

The writing tips in the upcoming section cover improving your writing generally and for inclusivity and accessibility. There are, however, a couple of items from the list above that need more specific recommendations, and I cover those after the general tips.

How to improve your writing

The following tips are some common steps I take to make writing more confident and easier to understand.

Consistency

Decide on the terminology you use to describe and identify certain terms and stick to it. Figure out your documentation's general tone of voice and stick to it. Every inconsistency you have leaves the reader wondering if you mean the same thing as you meant before. Does a distributed network consist of units, nodes, or instances? It doesn't matter which you pick, but once you do, stick to it. Once you settle on an example use case or more, stick to them and build upon them. Are you formal or friendly in your tone? Do you use humor (if you do, be careful, but that's another discussion)? Again, your decision isn't important at this level of discussion. What's important is that you stick to your decision.

Regarding terminology, technology is full of jargon and acronyms. That is, single-letter combinations of words (for example, UI, JSON, and API). Sometimes, we use them so often that I think many of us aren't even sure what they stand for anymore. For less common acronyms, and maybe even some of those less common than you might think, it's good practice to expand the acronym before you start using it.

Here's an example:

"This guide covers how to use our command-line interface (CLI)."

Similarly, if your chosen terminology or acronyms aren't standard, or you're unsure if they are standard, it's a good idea to start with or include a link to a terminology guide.

Chapter 6 covers style guides that take writing consistency to other levels, but initially, you can start with these basic decisions, and they help you define and create a style guide over time.

Involving the user

OK – now comes an actual grammar lesson masquerading as a conversation about user-focused content. I must try my best, you know. Look at these two explanations of a hypothetical product.

Here's example one:

"A result is returned by the function."

And this is example two:

"The function returns a result."

On the surface, they seem similar and explain the same concept, but they are different.

Example one uses what's called the *passive voice*, and example two uses what's called the *active voice*. You might have heard these concepts before, as they are spoken about often in some forms of writing, and much has been written and said about them. However, understanding the difference and, more importantly, what to change is sometimes complex.

It's easier to start by explaining active voice. With an active voice, you make the actor(s) and the subject(s) clear and specific. In many cases in technical documentation, and in the preceding example, the actor is the reader, but this is not always true. The actor could also be another function, a service, a company department, and so on. The subject is typically what the reader is interested in understanding – for example, *the function* in the example – but not always. The subject could also be another function, a service, another system, and so on.

And what is passive voice? The subject is often clear in passive voice, but generally not the actor.

Typically, with technical documentation, you should use active voice as much as possible. It involves the reader, making your writing sound more confident as the interactions and actions are clear to them. Passive voice can obscure details and make it unclear what is happening with what effect. Often, rephrasing a sentence into active voice also helps you to rethink in more detail how the components of a system fit together and understand it better from a user's perspective. However, it isn't always possible to make the actor(s) and subject(s) clear or making them clear makes a sentence more confusing. For example, in complex, distributed systems, where actors influence other actors, what happens in what order and when is unclear.

Stephen King's wonderful book *On Writing*, which is useful for writers of all flavors, contains many juicy quotes about confident grammar, especially active versus passive voice. He has this to say on the subject:

"Verbs come in two types, active and passive. With an active verb, the subject of the sentence is doing something.

With a passive verb, something is being done to the sentence's subject. The subject is just letting it happen. You should avoid the passive tense."

The reasons someone uses passive voice relate much to the points discussed earlier. It's easier to write in a passive voice for inexperienced writers. Personally, I tend to start with it in the first draft and switch to active voice in later drafts. It can be a more fluid way of writing. Marketing and product teams may push for using passive voice or at least start using it in any copy they contribute. This relates to some of my earlier points. Using passive voice can make you sound less responsible for something.

If you want a final example of why to avoid passive voice, think of a time you had to deal with some form of bureaucracy or service personnel. If you live in a non-English speaking country where passive and active language is less of an issue, this example might not fully apply, but I am sure you can at least identify with it.

How did they deal with and respond to you? It was probably in a distant and cold, non-committal way. Say, for example, you made an application request, and you received a response such as the following:

"Approval will be notified in due course."

What does that mean? When? By whom? This is an example of "passive-aggressive" communication, a wonderful term commonly used in British English to describe a way of communicating that is intentionally unclear and aggressive without sounding like it is.

Do you want your documentation to sound like that? I thought not! Then, try and use active voice.

Another classic quote from *On Writing* that really pushes the point about confident writing is this:

"*Many writers are attracted to passive verbs. The passive voice is safe. There is no troublesome action to contend with; the subject just has to close its eyes and think of England, to paraphrase Queen Victoria. I think unsure writers also feel the passive voice somehow lends their work authority, perhaps even a quality of majesty.*"

King then continues criticizing instruction manuals' writers, so stop there. Technical writing has improved its reputation in the 20+ years since he wrote the book, so forgive him for now.

Keeping it short

It's tempting to say "keep it simple" instead, but this is technical documentation and not always simple, and you should avoid using words such as "simple" anyway. However, just because what you are explaining is complex doesn't mean you need to write verbose and rambling text. Writing short, concise text is much harder than writing longer text.

There is a famous and often mis-accredited (Pascal, Locke, Franklin, Thoreau, Cicero, Wilson?) quote:

"*If I Had More Time, I Would Have Written a Shorter Letter*"

This could be because you are an inexperienced writer, and learning the skills to explain yourself concisely takes time and experience. It could also be because you don't understand what you're explaining as much as you think. I have always argued that you can summarize any concept, no matter how complex, into what's called an "elevator pitch" in the business world. That is a pitch that someone could hear during an elevator ride. Probably a couple of minutes at most. I imagine many technical people are reading this and thinking, "That's impossible. How could I possibly reduce my amazing, unique, and technically brilliant idea into a couple of minutes? I need hours!"

You don't.

Of course, that elevator pitch misses details – a lot of details. But that's OK. This is not something you even need to include in the documentation but is more of an exercise in getting you to think concisely. Start with what you are documenting to help people accomplish. When someone first encounters your project or product, that's all most people want to know to begin with. Then, they make their minds up to dig further from there.

Take **Kubernetes**, for example. It's an extremely complex and configurable tool, and if you wanted to explain everything it was possible to do with it, you would need a long amount of time. But an elevator pitch for Kubernetes could be something like the following:

"*An open source way for automating the running and management of large-scale applications to suit user needs.*"

Similarly, you can take that elevator pitch and expand explanations from there. Instead of starting writing from the technical nitty gritty, you start explaining from the simplest user-focused perspective.

This covers the conceptual ways to simplify and shorten your writing, but what about the technical how? Try the following tips.

Removing unnecessary words

English is a flexible language. You could put an English sentence in a blender, and it would still make sense at the end (I am sure this is a quote from somewhere, but I can't find the source). You can also cut many words from sentences, and they hold up just fine. Knowing which words to remove takes time and experience, but here are a few common candidates, often called "weasel words."

Beginning a sentence with the word "so"

It is often common in spoken language to indicate a pause or beginning of a phrase. It's typically unnecessary when used at the beginning of a sentence or phrase in written language, especially technical writing. It is still useful and valid in other contexts.

Here are some examples:

"*So, now you have the package installed.*"

"*Authenticate so that you can issue commands.*"

The "so" in the first example is unnecessary and has no purpose. In the second example, the "so" has more purpose and is OK, used as is, but you could still probably rewrite it in a clearer way.

Using words such as "simply," "easily," and "just"

Don't tell readers that something is easy or straightforward. Let them discover it themselves. If the reader finds that something isn't as "simple" or as "easy" as you said it was, that text makes them feel inferior or stupid, or perhaps it shows that your product or documentation doesn't work. Removing these words also helps you address inclusive language by reducing patronizing and unhelpful aspects of language.

Using the word "very"

Rarely needed in technical writing, "very" does nothing but accentuate something you have already said. While this can work in less formal language, narrative, or fiction writing, it isn't needed in technical writing. It can come across as over the top, "marketing speak," and – yes – unconfident. You don't need to tell someone something is "very fast." They will figure out if it is themselves, and if it turns out not "very fast," then your writing seems disingenuous.

Adverbs and adjectives

Most words that don't add value to documentation are examples of "adverbs" and "adjectives."

It's time for a short grammar lesson:

- A *verb* is a word that describes an action, state, or something that happened. It's often the main part of a sentence. For example, in "*The function returns value x*," the verb is "*returns*."
- A *noun* is a person, place, or thing. For example, "*function*" is a noun.
- An *adjective* is a word that describes a noun, for example, a "*complex function*."
- An *adverb* is a word or phrase that modifies or adds to an adjective or verb, for example, a "*very complex function*."

OK – with that summary out of the way, I can return to my main point. In technical English, you rarely need adverbs or adjectives. Generally, they only confirm something you have already said or add no value to what you need to say.

For example, does a reader need to know if a function is complex? Maybe they do, but they don't need to know that it's a very complex function. In those examples, "function" is a noun, "complex" is an adjective, and "very" is an adverb. The only word documentation usually needs is the noun.

I appreciate that recognizing an English sentence's various parts takes time and experience, but tools are available to help. *Chapter 8* covers some of these.

Another great quote from *On Writing*:

"*With adverbs, the writer usually tells us they aren't expressing themselves clearly, that they are not getting the point or the picture across.*"

Using shorter phrases and words

As you slowly cut "weasel" words, your text becomes shorter, but often, there are entire phrases you can replace with one word and lose maybe some nuance but little meaning. And technical writing isn't about nuance but clear, concise language.

Classic examples are some of the following:

- "*to*" instead of "*in order to*". Most of the time, "*to*" does the job, but sometimes "*in order to*" can show more purpose or motivation, but this isn't often relevant with tech writing.
- "*Most*" instead of "*Almost all*."
- "*Now*" instead of "*At the present time*."
- "*Often*" instead of" In *many cases*."
- "*Sometimes*" instead of "*In some cases*."

There are many other "weasel" words (not all commonly used in technical writing anyway). Some of the the tools covered in *Chapter 9* help will help you identify these words, but for more comprehensive lists, try the following links:

- `https://dianaurban.com/words-you-should-cut-from-your-writing-immediately`
- `https://www.brandeis.edu/writing-program/resources/faculty/handouts/four-types-unnecessary-words-phrases.html`
- `https://blog.wordvice.com/avoid-fillers-powerful-writing/`

Don't show off – let the product speak for itself

At the risk of repeating myself, many documentation readers aren't native English speakers, so using overly complex language and phrases likely confuses them as they try to accomplish their goals. Documentation isn't the place to show off your English skills. The same applies to native English speakers, who need to be especially careful not to overuse cultural references and colloquialisms that are not only unfamiliar to non-native speakers but are equally unfamiliar to native English speakers from other countries.

Documentation is also not the place to show off how good you think your product or programming skills are. If you need a place to do that, save it for a blog post.

From an inclusivity perspective, "showing off" can add to rude, negative, or unhelpful language. While not common, I have come across documentation that makes dismissive assumptions about the readers' education or technical level that comes across as arrogant and thus rude.

I know I have disappointed many writers when I have chopped and changed all the wonderful prose they spent hours crafting, but again, the reader is the most important person.

Don't repeat yourself

There are certain things worth repeating in tech writing and certain things you don't need to repeat.

You don't need to repeat something you just said to make a point. Again, this comes back to confident writing. If a reader just learned that authenticating with your API is "easy," you don't need to tell them again.

Here's an example (and there are a few things wrong with this example to illustrate the point):

"Get your access key from the control panel in the top-left corner of the dashboard to authenticate with the API. Now you have your API key, you can authenticate with the API."

However, it is worth repeating yourself to summarize what the reader has learned in a section or page. As the next chapter covers, page structure also aids understanding and documentation. Readers often don't read pages from start to finish, so regularly summarizing sections helps a reader know what they should know but might have scrolled past.

Inclusive language: in more detail

I promised to revisit the topic of using more inclusive language that didn't fit into some of the more general advice. The following sections cover this, but practically speaking, you can consider more inclusive writing to be generally better writing.

Overly negative language

Unnecessary negativity is rarely found in documentation but not completely unheard of. Documentation is not the place for opinions on your product or anyone else's. It isn't the place to criticize certain approaches or technical decisions or give your opinions on software development or the tech industry. It's certainly not the place to make the reader feel inferior. It's a place to help people learn how to use something. If you have opinions to share, save them for a personal blog post, podcast, or video.

Another less obvious use of negative language to avoid is when describing what the reader can and can't do with what you're documenting. If you have any kind of relationship with a marketing team, they're likely to push your writing in the complete opposite direction. If you don't, it is possible to slowly slide into a negative viewpoint. What do I mean? I mean that your writing should be from the perspective of what the reader can do instead of what they can't do, for example:

"You can't use the account page to reset your password. Contact support instead."

Instead, try something more positive, such as the following:

"To reset your password, contact support. Use the account page to update your email address and username."

Biased language

We are full of biases built upon a lifetime of societal, cultural, and personal experiences. Most of them probably won't find their way into documentation, but some will, and ideally, you should remove as many as possible that do. This book isn't the place for a lengthy discussion on why you should do this, but in short, it removes as much potential for offense as possible. Removing biased language has little actual effect on the effectiveness of your documentation, so why not do it anyway?

Gender

Unlike many other common languages, English is mostly a non-gendered language in that inanimate objects don't need a gender. A table is a table. It isn't male, female, neutral, or any other gendered identity. While this makes it easier to remove gender from English text, it can still sneak in. First, some non-native speakers sometimes assign a gender to inanimate objects, for example:

"The API, he responds with x"

In English, that gender isn't necessary.

A far more common unnecessary use of gender is when referring to animate objects – that is, people.

First, when referring to individuals, there has traditionally been a difference of opinion between US and non-US English on this topic.

Typically, in non-US English, you can use "they/them" almost anywhere to avoid using gender when referring to an animate actor. Traditionally, this was grammatically incorrect as it's supposed to refer to a group of people, but being the flexible language it is, English has grown to accept this as correct.

US English tends to pick a gender from a length of text, use it, and then maybe switch to another, and so on, generally attempting to balance gender usage. However, I see this approach used less in writing overall and almost never in documentation. So, for this chapter's purposes, I can confidently say use "they/them" if you need to refer to an animate actor, singular or plural.

Your options become more nuanced when referring to a collective of people, especially when using terminology, we have grown used to using to refer to a job or role in general. It's uncommon for you to use these that much in documentation, but still, it's worth drawing attention to anyway.

Here's an example:

"The service operates like a middleman, passing status messages to other services."

You should replace "middleman" with something without a gender, for example, "intermediary."

Probably the most common offender – again, not used much in documentation – is "guys." The argument over whether this term has transcended gender to mean something else is ongoing, but it's one of my daily irritants, and I'm writing this chapter, so there it is. There are plenty of far better alternatives, such as "everyone," "folks," or "all."

Out-of-date language

Far more common is the use of out-of-date, possibly even considered offensive language. What constitutes this is an evolving discussion. But here are some examples.

To show some examples, I need to use words that some might find offensive. It's also worth noting that changing some of the terminology might be out of your direct control if that's a term the product uses. But if so, take a copy of this book and show it to someone who can.

For example, instead of "*Disable the configuration option*," it's better to use *toggle, turn off, change,* and so on, depending on the use case.

Another classic computing term that still sparks much discussion around its usage is *master* and *slave* in relation to distributed systems. I don't want to get too deep into discussions over this problematic pair of terms but suffice it to say, they have a loaded history and plenty of alternatives.

You can try "follower" and "leader," which still has some issues but is better. "Primary" and "replica" is a much better alternative. It's also worth thinking if you need these terms at all. Without digging into the technical details of distributed systems, an increasing number of distributed systems use more fluid hierarchical approaches.

Another problematic word pairing is "*black list*" and "*white list*," and the arguments for and against are similar to the aforementioned terms. However, in this case, the alternatives are more decided upon, with "deny list" and "allow list."

That's an example of three words or phrases with better, more contemporary alternatives, but there are far more.

Here are some links and further resources on the topic and examples of other terms to add more context to the discussion:

- `https://www.zdnet.com/article/linux-team-approves-new-terminology-bans-terms-like-blacklist-and-slave/`
- `https://www.zdnet.com/article/github-to-replace-master-with-alternative-term-to-avoid-slavery-references/`
- `https://inclusivenaming.org/word-lists/`

Summary

Grammar is a subject you could study your entire life and still be learning. This chapter gave you some building blocks for the most important aspects you need to know for technical writing. Remember the fundamental things you are trying to improve for your readers with good grammar choices:

- Remove as much of their cognitive load as possible when trying to understand complex or new topics
- Give the reader confidence that what they are reading is the best practice around a product and that the product can help them accomplish their goals

- Make it as clear as possible to readers how to accomplish a task they want to understand

- Make language as inclusive and unbiased as possible to broaden your audience and make them feel welcome

The next chapter looks at taking these grammatical building blocks and assembling them into a well-constructed page. Well-written words remain unread if they are presented poorly, hard to read, and hard to find.

4

Page Structure and How It Aids Reading

Chapter 3 covered crafting better words to help people understand what you want to explain. Have you ever attempted to read and understand something complex to be faced with a solid wall of text that's hard to parse to the point where your eyes stop processing any potentially fantastic information?

Crafting the perfect words is a waste of time if you make it extremely hard for anyone to read them. Thankfully, the principles of good layout for print and web-based output are well established, and documentarians can learn much from them to improve their content layout. In addition to these time-honored principles, there are a couple of other documentation and technical writing-specific tips worth considering, making things easier for your readers.

This chapter covers the following main topics:

- Humans are not your only readers
- The principles of good layout
- A primer on markup languages for the web
- Thinking about pages semantically
- Creating documentation menus and navigation

But before beginning with the tips, let's begin with who reads documentation or, more precisely, what reads it.

Humans are not your only readers

Unless you put in a lot of work to block them, likely, one of your documentation's largest consumers isn't humans. "Traditionally," this was search engine crawlers building an index of your documentation. In the past two years or so, this traffic now includes companies trawling material on publicly available sites to train **large language models (LLMs)** for **artificial intelligence (AI)** tools. As you will see later in this chapter and *Chapters 8* to *9*, this isn't necessarily a bad thing, as it offers people new interaction options with documentation. By following the structure tips in this chapter, when you improve the structure for human eyes, you improve it for machine consumers, too.

One final advantage of good structure is for humans who use additional hardware or software to consume content – that is, those who use screen readers for reading page content out loud, typically due to poor vision. While those who don't use them might be able to infer meaning from a lack of good layout, a machine reader will quickly get confused. In short, a good structure and layout help everyone!

The principles of good layout

Most rules for good page structure are similar to those for good HTML or web page structure. Some of this is because a lot of documentation is consumed as web pages, and the roots of good web page structure originate in decades, if not centuries, of best practices for non-digital and digital printing layout tools. Despite this long and venerable history and the proven benefits of using layout best practices, it's amazing how many tools, site builders, and sites don't conform to them. So, with this knowledge in hand, you can be that person who gets to fix everything.

Still with me? Good – you like to help!

Good modern layout principles begin with thinking about semantics. Traditionally, this involves using the correct heading and sub-heading levels to indicate structure. It involves using paragraph breaks when relevant, tables to present data, and so on. But more recently, to reflect the modern web, "semantic" markup means a lot more.

A quick primer on the markup language of the web

Without turning this book into a lesson on web development, **HTML** stands for **Hyper Text Markup Language**. Every web browser has a suite of tools for web developers, but even without those, you can view the page's source to see it differently. What you see when you do is an example of a *markup language*. HTML is a series of *tags* that surround page elements. These different tags mean different things.

For example, the <p> tag denotes a paragraph:

```
<p>A paragraph of text.</p>
```

Similarly, the `<b>` tab is used for bold text:

```
<b>Text in bold</b>
```

You don't need to worry too much about what's happening behind the scenes as a documentarian, as most tools handle the conversion between how you write and HTML for you. However, it's good to have a basic understanding of what's happening, as often, working as a solo documentarian involves a lot of customizing tools. So, you need to understand HTML.

However, tags such as `<p>` and `<b>` are old, originating long before the web. What's new in terms of semantic thinking are tags such as `<main>`, `<aside>`, and `<footer>`. While things such as `<p>` and `<b>` render in ways you can probably expect by default, these new semantic tags won't render in any particular way. However, many tools and site builders, including those *Chapter 6* covers, now do. Also, many other integrations and tools, such as screen readers, recognize these tags for what they mean and treat them semantically differently.

In the case of the tags mentioned previously, they generally imply the following:

- `<main>`: The dominant content area of a page
- `<aside>`: A portion of the page related to the content in `<main>`
- `<footer>`: Information about the content in an area such as `<main>`, such as author and copyright

I appreciate that my explanation sounds vague, and semantic markup is. What this markup means to tools that know how to handle it is to "treat these page elements this way," but what the tool does with it and how other tools render it is largely up to the tool and/or you.

What does this all mean to a documentarian? I am encouraging you to think semantically when you write. Not only is page structure important, but it's what most modern tools and browsers expect. Let's start at the beginning with a page title.

Thinking about pages semantically

Any web page – in fact, most pages in any format – begin with a title or heading. Regarding HTML, this should be an `<h1></h1>` heading or heading level 1. Every page should have only one h1, but unfortunately, many tools and people break this rule to the page's detriment.

Typically, right after an h1 is some opening text, and then every following subheading should be an h2. Then, every subheading underneath is an h2, an h3, and so on. Most browsers comfortably handle everything down to an h5, and theoretically, you could keep going further down the levels. However, if you have that many subheadings, your content probably needs reorganizing.

Break up paragraphs as much as possible by a group of topics or a few sentences at a time. Don't fear whitespace. It helps people read and guide their eyes around a page. This is the same with subheadings. They break up the wall of text and draw people's eyes to important information.

Think about the last time you read a web page, especially one you used to find particular information, such as a page of documentation. Did you read it from top to bottom, left to right, taking in all the content? Or did you scroll and scan, looking for the snippets of information you needed?

I am almost certain that for most of you, it was the latter. Documentation is not a book. Well, a book can be documentation, but I think you see my point. People rarely read documentation from start to finish, at least not in the past 10 years or so since printed manuals became less common. This is why you need to structure the page with plenty of whitespace and page elements to draw people's attention to the most important information. Don't bury key details in large paragraphs. Make sure they stand out in balance with these elements that draw people's attention.

Chapter 7 covers more of these non-text elements in detail, but this includes images, code snippets, tables, GIFs, and anything else that breaks up a wall of text.

Lists

One common, simpler way of breaking up blocks of text is using lists to summarize or group small pieces of information. There are two types of lists: unordered lists, sometimes known as "bullet points," and ordered lists, sometimes known as "numbered lists."

Use an ordered list if something is a series of short steps that someone needs to follow in sequence. If you feel some steps need sub-steps, include those underneath each relevant step, but try not to get too many sub-levels deep, or it can get confusing for people to read and follow.

If something is a series of items and the ordering is less important, use an unordered list, again including a reasonable number of sub-bullets if need be.

Let's look at an example of a numbered list.

To start using Monito, follow these steps:

1. Get an access code:

    I. Create an account.

    II. Add your payment details.

    III. Click **Get access code** and copy the value.

    IV. Add the access code to environment variables.

2. Install Monito.

3. Run Monito.

Now, let's look at an example of a bulleted list.

Monito offers the following features:

- Customizable alerts
- Configurable metadata
- A data exporter

Paragraph breaks

While bullet points and numerical lists can help break up walls of text, don't overuse them or feel that all paragraphs should be short.

This is a trend that's quite popular now.

Especially in clickbait blogs.

And **Search Engine Optimization** (**SEO**) farm content, full of links that tell you nothing.

I guess it works well for algorithms or catching people's attention.

But over time, it's annoying to read.

And I apologize for doing that to you to make my point! I promise not to do it again.

Sometimes, a page doesn't need a lot of extra elements, or they serve no purpose beyond breaking up a wall of text. In this case, you can create space with paragraph line breaks. There are different opinions on how often to start new paragraphs, but typically around 100 to 200 words, or 5 to 6 sentences, is what you should aim for. But in practicality, a paragraph should gather the sentences and words most relevant to the topic or sub-topic at hand and let that guide the length more than anything. But if you can try to chunk your information together so that paragraphs don't become too long, that helps with readability.

Now, let's return to the topic of semantic markup. Many documentation tools offer features to break up text further and mark it as semantically relevant. Let's take a closer look at some of them.

Tables

One of the simplest semantic markup elements you can use is a table, but it's easy to overuse and misuse. Before the modern era of web development, people used to use tables for layout. Among some of us older web developers, there's sometimes a tendency to still think of them that way. A table is meant for organizing and displaying information. Typically, this is with rows representing a changing variable and columns showing data related to that variable.

An obvious use case for tables is comparing file sizes, speeds, and minimum dependency versions of releases.

A less obvious use case is a feature matrix of what's available in the SDKs you maintain.

However, many other components are common in documentation and documentation tools that may not be as familiar to you.

Admonitions

One common example is "admonitions" (my preferred term), "alerts," or "callouts." One non-agreed term for the same thing. A small, marked area of text denotes additional information relevant to the current topic. Depending on the tool, you can typically denote an admonition as one of the following types, which results in the following formatting:

- **Info**: Additional information that could interest the reader but isn't essential to know, such as background details or history. Different tools render this in different colors, typically gray or blue.

- **Note**: Note and information might sound similar, but they are more for supplemental information that is useful to some people in some situations – for example, if you use a network proxy, an unusual processor architecture, and so on. Different tools render this in different colors, typically gray or blue.

- **Tip**: Information that could be useful to most people but not essential. An example could be updating dependencies before installing one specific to the project. It's typically rendered in green.

- **Caution or warning**: Information that's somewhat important for most people to see – for example, to ensure the reader is connected to the right network before issuing a command. It's typically rendered in yellow or orange.

- **Error or danger**: Information that's essential for people to notice and read – for example, not reading could cause data loss, high costs, and so on. It's typically rendered in red.

The following figure shows how the **Docusaurus** tool renders admonitions by default:

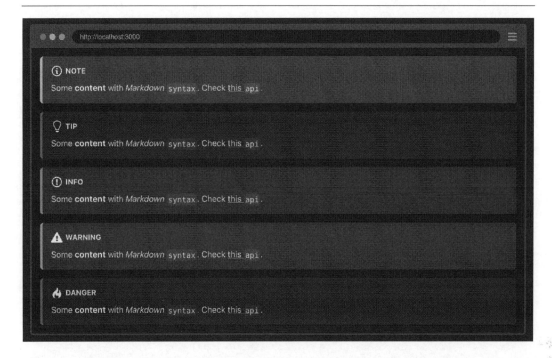

Figure 4.1 – An example of rendered admonitions from the Docusaurus tool

Some tools provide other admonition types, but the ones I've covered here are the most commonly available and used. Used sparingly, admonitions make information stand out, but if you find yourself using three in a row, you have only replaced a wall of text with a wall of admonitions, which has not solved the problem, and you probably need to reorganize your content.

Tabs

Another classic layout component in documentation is tabs, which let you group related information together that might not be relevant to every reader. For example, you have similar installation steps for Windows, macOS, and Linux in a Getting Started guide. It's unlikely that everyone wants to read all three, so you can segment each instruction set using tabs, keeping the content in the same source file and page but allowing people to toggle between what matters to them.

The following screenshot shows a code tab and a content tab from the **Material for MKDocs** theme:

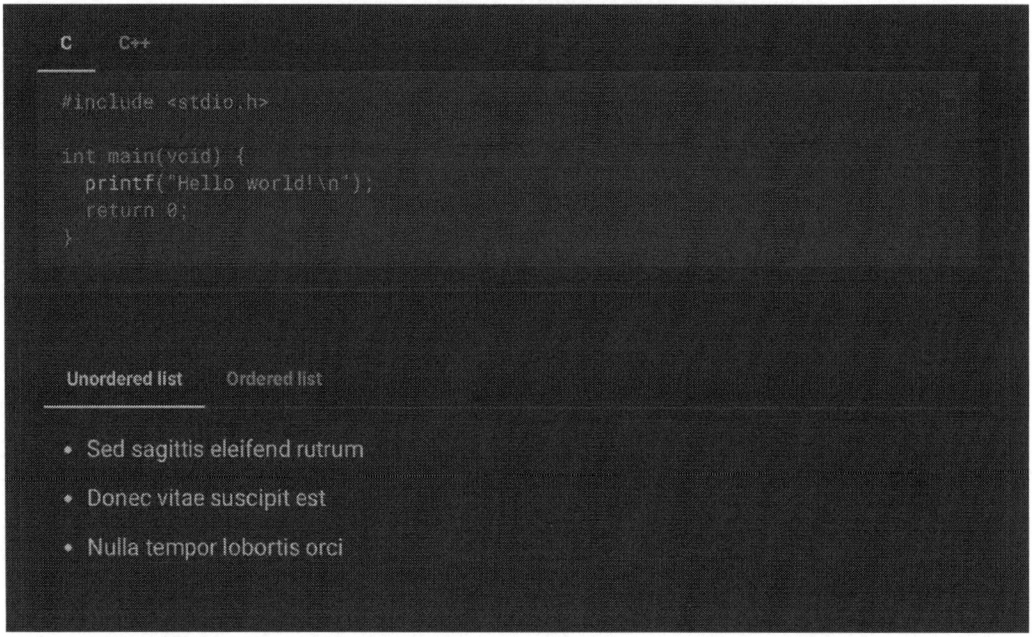

Figure 4.2 – A code tab and a content tab from the Material for MKDocs theme

Not all tools support tabs, and they implement them in different ways. However, they are a fairly common content organizational tool and, again, something people's eyes notice as they scroll around.

An example of a well-structured page

Continuing to use the Monito example, here's a Skeleton of how I might structure a Getting Started page with plenty of headings, code tabs, admonitions, and more:

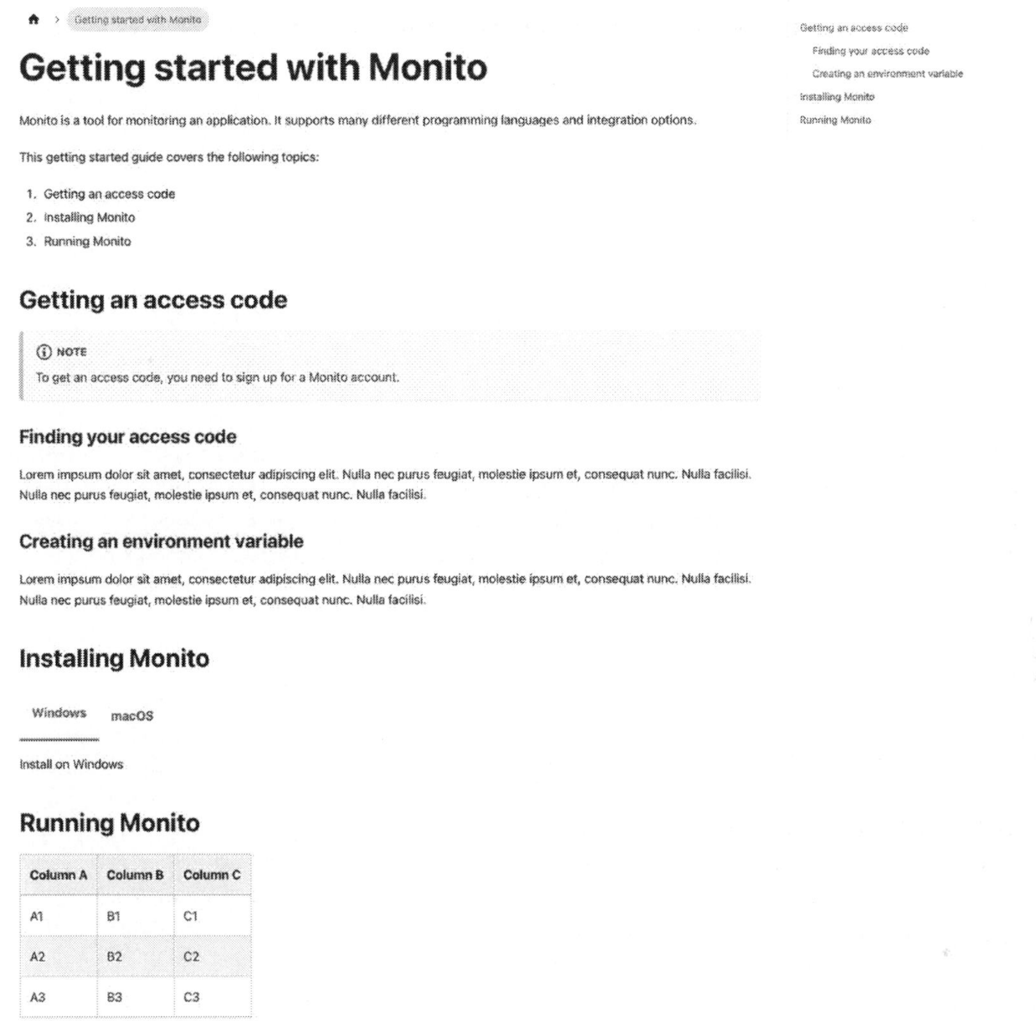

♠ > Getting started with Monito

Getting started with Monito

Monito is a tool for monitoring an application. It supports many different programming languages and integration options.

This getting started guide covers the following topics:

1. Getting an access code
2. Installing Monito
3. Running Monito

Getting an access code

> ⓘ **NOTE**
> To get an access code, you need to sign up for a Monito account.

Finding your access code

Lorem impsum dolor sit amet, consectetur adipiscing elit. Nulla nec purus feugiat, molestie ipsum et, consequat nunc. Nulla facilisi. Nulla nec purus feugiat, molestie ipsum et, consequat nunc. Nulla facilisi.

Creating an environment variable

Lorem impsum dolor sit amet, consectetur adipiscing elit. Nulla nec purus feugiat, molestie ipsum et, consequat nunc. Nulla facilisi. Nulla nec purus feugiat, molestie ipsum et, consequat nunc. Nulla facilisi.

Installing Monito

Windows   macOS

Install on Windows

Running Monito

Column A	Column B	Column C
A1	B1	C1
A2	B2	C2
A3	B3	C3

Figure 4.3 – A layout showing an example of a well-structured page

Creating documentation menus and navigation

So far, I've spoken about how to organize the content of individual pages but not about how to organize entire pages. How do you structure a collection of documentation pages?

This is a hard topic, and not even an experienced technical writing team has all the answers to it. Fortunately, most tools let you move and rearrange content structures relatively easily, so it's typically an ongoing experiment rather than something set in stone.

If you ask users what they want in terms of document site navigation, the answer is typically one large Google-style search box, as in truth, no one is sure what sort of navigation would help them find what they want and achieve the same for everyone else. If you ask different team members or teams, you'd probably end up with a menu with a long list of all the content. So, in reality, documentation site navigation is a continual experiment, at best consisting of compromises built around some standard patterns.

Following menu patterns

One important factor to remember is that readers often don't arrive at pages in documentation directly. They often find them from search engine results, links on third-party websites, and, possibly from now on, from source links in AI-powered chatbots.

My point is that people probably won't follow your carefully considered and constructed navigation all the time anyway, and often, they find themselves on random pages. This means that no matter where people are in your documentation structure, you also need to consider showing them the ideal path as to how someone might arrive at that page. What are the ideal steps they should have followed before reading the page they ended up at?

To begin with, navigation and structure can follow similar patterns to the content types covered in *Chapter 2*:

- QuickStart
- Guides
- Reference

Here, each sub-section and page follows under those loose sections. Try to use gerund-style verbs – that is, those that end with "-ing" or that give the impression of "doing" something. Building on the content needed, as identified in *Chapter 2*. Here's the list again:

- QuickStart
- SDKs:
  - Python
  - Go
  - JavaScript
  - Ruby
  - C++

- Features:

  - Hosted dashboard

  - Advanced alerting

  - Conditional alerting

  - Creating custom metadata

- Self-hosting:

  - Docker

  - Kubernetes

  - Bare-metal

- Integrations:

  - Alerting tools

  - Alternative backends

  - Exporting data

These are OK titles for pages. They say what they are and are to the point, but if you wanted to rephrase them in gerund-style titles, they could be as follows:

- Getting started with Monito

- Building with Monito SDKs:

  - Integrating with Python

  - Integrating with Go

  - Integrating with JavaScript

  - Integrating with Ruby

  - Integrating with C++

- Adding features:

  - Using the hosted dashboard

  - Adding advanced alerting

  - Adding conditional alerting

  - Creating custom metadata

- Self-hosting Monito:

  - Using Docker

  - Using Kubernetes

  - Running on bare-metal

- Integrating Monito:

  - Connecting alerting tools

  - Adding alternative backends

  - Exporting data

This is a good starting point for a structure. The balance is having content organized to a point where readers can identify what they will learn without breaking the documentation into so many pages that they have to click multiple times to find anything.

Getting this right will take time and experimentation based on feedback and metrics. It won't happen immediately, and that's OK. Documentation is typically a loose collection of content files you can move around. It's not a book where having the content structure locked in place before release is more crucial.

Adding internal search

You should add an internal search to documentation to help fill those times when it may not be obvious to someone where to find what they're looking for, especially in a reference section. Read *Chapter 6* and *Chapter 9* for further discussion on what tools you can use. This chapter covers the principles. You do not have to reinvent Google to add search to documentation. Many free and commercial tools have existed to help for a long time. You can add metadata to content (again, *Chapter 6* covers that in more detail) to handle related terms people might search for that don't directly map to the content of a page. If you follow the earlier advice in this chapter, you're already helping search, both internal and external. To reiterate, good content and page structure that follows expected standards and rules help machine and human readers.

Keeping links working

I mentioned earlier that the nature of documentation means you may regularly rearrange content. The web is built on interconnected pages, and we all know how frustrating it can be to encounter a broken link. Also, search engines tend to penalize sites with broken links, downranking the site in search results. Documentation's main purpose is to inform, not sell, but still, as many potential readers will find your content via search engines, it's good practice to keep links functioning as much as possible. Different tools and services offer different ways to do this or check if there are links you need to update.

Regarding internal links, this is an appropriate place to return to the topic of markup, HTML, and the often misunderstood topic of link text.

How often have you seen a link with the text **Click here**? Quite a lot, I imagine. Maybe you've even created a few yourself.

I heard a quote from someone that said, *"click here," "click," "more," or "read more" link text was comparable to shops having signs that just said "shop."* It only tells you what you already know and nothing about what will happen when you click the link (or enter the shop).

Link text should be as descriptive as page titles and menu entries. Aim for link text that's at least 3 to 5 words long and describes what the reader gets from clicking the link.

Here are some examples in documentation:

- *"How to configure Monito"*
- *"The full list of configuration options"*

Using meaningful link text helps human readers, but guess what? Returning to a theme, it also helps non-human readers. I cover aspects of accessibility throughout this book, but many people with poor vision use a screen reader for some description. Screen readers read page elements out to people, but imagine hearing the following over and over again:

"**Link**. Click. **Link**. Click. **Link**. More."

If that's not enough to motivate you, search engines also use link text to build an index of what links lead where and what to expect. What do you think "click here" says to a search engine? Not much.

The H and T in HTML stand for Hyper Text, and "Hyper Links," or, as we now know them, "links," were the main purpose of the web's invention. Keeping them helpful for all keeps the web, and especially documentation, as helpful as possible to everyone.

Summary

This chapter looked at how to make your wonderful words readable to all interested in consuming them. It looked at how you can use simpler and more complex page elements to add space and context to the information it presents.

If there are two pieces of advice to take away from this chapter, they are as follows:

- Your content needs to be readable as well as well-written
- There are many more readers of your documentation in addition to human eyes

With some underpinning practical techniques in place, the next chapter looks at the process you must follow to start and continue writing.

5
The Technical Writing Process

In the previous two chapters, you learned how to structure documentation pages and grammar and style fundamentals for effective communication. With this knowledge, you're now ready to tackle this chapter, which covers the process of working with others to figure out what to document and how effective it is.

The process of creating technical documentation isn't too dissimilar to the process of creating the code that documentation explains. Creating technical documentation is never "done" or "finished" and is a constant iterative learning and improvement process.

The stages of the process, as I see them, are also fairly similar to software engineering. This chapter covers the following main topics:

- Scoping and requirements gathering
- Research and product testing
- Drafting and re-drafting
- Feedback, testing, and maintenance

These steps apply when creating new content or content for new features but can also apply when fixing issues or tweaking existing content, just minus some steps, or much shorter steps.

Scoping and requirements gathering

Within a company or project, documentation requests can come from a variety of internal and external sources, including the following:

- A new feature that's in progress, probably from a product owner
- A new feature that's already been completed that needs documentation
- A feature gap that's been identified by you or others

- A content gap that's been identified by you or others
- A problem that's been logged by you or others

When you start filling that content need, the first step is to figure out the current definition of done. I say "current" as just because there may be a completion point for the content needed now doesn't mean it will remain that way forever. Likely, it will not be considered done in the future. However, while there are predictable potential future changes, there are also others that aren't, and finishing the work as completely as possible now can save work in the future.

"Done" is a complicated concept and one that different people have different opinions of and on, which is why it's important to define it as clearly as possible from different perspectives. It's worth noting that, try as hard as you might, you may still find that what you thought everyone meant by "done" is not how things turn out when you think you're "done." Depending on the people you work with and the type of company or project you work on, how you must mitigate this happening can vary, but I provide some tips and advice based on my experience.

Ask stakeholders what their expectations for the content is. These questions vary:

- An engineer might want you to cover important technical aspects they feel are essential for a user to know.
- A product owner might want you to cover how a new feature helps users save time with their daily work.
- Someone in a marketing team might want you to cover how the feature compares to competitors' feature sets. Any other content creators might want you to write about the feature in a particular way.

You need to dig deeper than these one-line summaries of each stakeholder's potential requirements, probably asking the same question in different ways or asking clarifying questions. Someone in one of those roles might supply you with other content that gives you some of the details you need or that you can base follow-up questions on.

While it can sometimes take several rounds of questions to dig into these expectations, people are usually clearer about them than their assumptions. What are their assumptions? Well, that's hard to say. Often they won't say them at all:

- An engineer might assume that anyone reading the content knows a key technical detail when they don't, perhaps because they were too deep into the code of the feature and didn't see the bigger picture or assumed that all other engineers "must know this"
- A product owner might assume a certain flow for the content because they have been focused on an ideal user flow for someone using the feature
- Someone in marketing might assume that you will describe the feature in overly positive and sales-heavy language and not in terms of practical usage

Another content creator might assume that you will write in a particular style or layout that you haven't been made aware of.

Directly asking, "What are your assumptions about their content?" might not unearth them, but learning about the kinds of assumptions that each stakeholder might make can help you ask questions about those assumptions.

What to document

If you are starting an entire set of documentation or a major feature from scratch, you might be wondering what to work on first and how much documentation you need.

At the risk of repeating myself, documentation is an iterative process, especially if you are a small team or undertaking documentation as part of another role. It's almost impossible for you to document everything that a product might need at once. Unless you work in a sector where completeness and full accuracy are essential at launch, such as medical, sensitive industrial, and so on, then it's unlikely you need everything documented at once.

So, where do you start? And how do you proceed after you start? If you have some existing metrics or roadmap that informs you of an order to document a product, then follow it, but in reality, it's unlikely you will have any existing guidance, and it's mostly "up to you."

My general advice is to start at the beginning, then the end, and slowly fill in the gaps in the middle over time based on feedback.

This means creating a getting started guide or two and then ensuring that reference documentation is available to cover resources such as API or SDK functions. With these in place, you can release "minimum viable documentation." The getting started guides will be enough for those who are interested in experimenting with a product to see if it suits their needs, and the reference documentation will be enough for those who know what they want to accomplish and need more details on the individual components to use.

With that content in place, you can use product roadmaps, further drafting phases, and the metrics you gather over time to fill in the gaps, slowly reaching toward "more complete documentation."

Research and product testing

If you are documenting something technical, then there is no replacement for getting your hands dirty experimenting with and using a product like an end user might do. This process is easier if you have a technical background or experience, but you can gain that over time, and sometimes, having a fresh pair of eyes can help reveal problems no one had anticipated. In small companies, at least, documentarians are often the first people to try a product or feature after developers, and our position between engineering, product, marketing, and support can give us a unique and broad perspective on a product.

However, I am what I call a "technical" tech writer. I studied computer science. I dabble in programming. I can throw together infrastructure as code and databases quite happily. Don't ask me to create a large-scale production-ready application, but I know enough to write examples and, crucially, ask the right questions.

Few documentarians specialize in documenting one product, project, or ecosystem in their entire career. As hard as you might try (and we tend to have curious minds), you can't learn and understand everything about any product, project, or ecosystem, and not more than one of these. But again, to reiterate, what documentarians do have is a broad overview of many things, sometimes more than anyone else. It's the nature of creating documentation. You need to know how components fit together to form a flow, even if you're a writer on a team.

This means that documentarians need to learn how to learn, what questions to ask, where to probe, and how to figure out the important bits and pieces that are essential to explaining a concept. This process leads from asking team members and collaborators questions to asking questions about the product itself. You can then take this knowledge and hands-on experience and ask team members better and more informed questions during review processes.

You can achieve this experience and exposure by watching demos and speaking with the team members who built it, but nothing replaces trying it yourself.

This book is primarily aimed at engineers who want to increase their documentation skills, but there will likely be people from other backgrounds and even experienced engineers reading. Well, sometimes, they assume knowledge of their own and others.

While this varies from product to product, my process for learning to learn a product is roughly as follows.

The first step – almost step zero – is to assume nothing about the end user. This sounds obvious, but we all bring many biases and assumptions from our knowledge and experiences that vary wildly, from operating system choice to educational background, all of which can affect how we might explain something to someone. Over time, you build an internal list to check. Here are some ideas:

- The operating system used, including its version and architecture, as well as any security restrictions in place from an IT team.
- Common dependencies such as version control systems and language runtime versions.

A quick aside about surprising dependencies

I have lost hours trying to install JavaScript dependencies that relied on a Python or C dependency, with no mention of this anywhere in the documentation. You need to check *all* dependencies!

- Programming language norms and patterns that are common to the language the application is written in but not necessarily for end users

- Your common process for setting up a project or environment

If the project involves the user undertaking some kind of environment setup to run a programming language or database, for example, then some tools can help you start from a clean setup each time. Without getting into too much detail, look into container runtime technologies such as Docker or Podman. These tools let you define a set of configurations around an application and start it isolated from the rest of your machine, meaning you won't detrimentally affect the rest of your local machine. When you're done, you can delete the instance of that application and recreate and delete it as you need. Other options to consider are programming language version managers, which let you switch between different versions as relevant for projects. One final option is using a virtual machine, a completely separate "computer" and operating system running on your computer. This can be useful if you want to test software on Windows when you're using macOS, for example.

If you're testing software that runs in isolation, such as in a web browser or desktop application, then find out if there's a way to reset it to its defaults so that you can repeatedly test as a new user would.

There are also ways to have a development or operations team set up reproducible environments for you, meaning you can have a setup that regularly refreshes itself.

With the underpinnings in place for testing and learning, how do you learn? Like learning in general, often, it's easier when you have a practical project to try and learn from. Often, creating such a project is also useful, and it also helps to have code in the documentation and downloadable demo projects. If you don't have a personal project in mind or one that suits the project, ask teams in the company that might, such as customer support, customer success, sales engineers, or developer relations.

Take that application, start it, break it, experiment with it, and try to integrate it with other services and tools. Use it like an end user would. If you can access the code, dig into it and look around to see how it fits together.

You won't understand everything, and you don't need to. This experimentation just helps you ask better and more informed questions.

Drafting and re-drafting

Now, it's time to start writing. Much like any other form of writing, one draft is rarely enough. Once you have a first draft, you need to get all involved stakeholders to take a look and give their input. This process can take some time, but it is important to ensure the correct balance of technical accuracy, company priorities, and language clarity.

This chapter won't focus on tools for doing this, but the process. There are several well-established toolchains for reviewing technical copy that influence the advice I give, but I try to remain as agnostic as possible.

Getting rounds of feedback on documentation can directly correlate to your ability to extract the expectations and assumptions mentioned earlier. If these were not clear in the earlier stages, then this likely becomes evident during feedback. Sometimes, this is because you misunderstood or incorrectly assumed something communicated with you, or more often than not because people are often not sure of themselves until they see something in front of them.

I have found that feedback on documentation comes at two extremes: next to no feedback to the point that you're unsure what anyone thought, or so much feedback you don't know where to start. You must deal with both cases in different ways.

If you don't receive enough, you may need to set up specific sessions to get feedback from stakeholders. When faced with walls of text or a list of changes, people aren't sure how they feel about it, so you need to ask specific questions. With a lot of user testing, you generally don't want to lead the user, but content is different as you risk getting lots of feedback about details you may not need feedback on at this point or complaints about the product or feature.

Here are some potential questions to ask:

- What did you think about what you read?
- If you could change anything about what you read, what would it be?
- What was easy or difficult to understand and why?
- How would you explain this content to someone else?
- Does this address your needs? If not, why not?

If you have clear competitors with similar feature documentation, ask similar questions about that content.

As you ask these questions and receive answers, people are also likely to give feedback that, while it's useful, you didn't need at this point – things such as word choice and grammar and spelling issues. Some of these may be genuine mistakes, while others have reasons for being the way they are. But for the most part, these are a distraction in the early stages of review. You want subject matter experts to give you feedback on their area of expertise, not a misplaced comma. Of course, when you get feedback from other writers, then worry about these misplaced commas, but as I say, you want each subject expert to give feedback on their area of expertise as much as possible.

Too much feedback doesn't necessarily mean you did a bad job. Some reviewers are opinionated or have lots of thoughts they want to share. The harder part of too much feedback is going through it and figuring out what to do with it.

Some of it will be useful and similar to what I mentioned previously, but it might not focus on what you need feedback on from that person. Make a note of it for a later day and politely thank the reviewer for their comment. Some of it might just be thoughts they wanted to share on the product, feature, or documentation they feel is needed regarding a related concept. Again, make a note of it for a later day and thank the reviewer for their feedback. What's left will be varying levels of usefulness, and likely, much of it will be contradictory feedback. Your job is to sift through all that feedback and determine what you want to act on and when. As a documentarian, you may not be the expert on the product's inner workings, but you are an expert on figuring out how to explain them. It's OK to push back on feedback, but do it in a friendly, professional manner and explain why you choose not to accept it.

Sometimes, that's enough for a reviewer to accept your counter-feedback, but sometimes, it's not. It's all too easy for rounds of feedback to get heated, especially when it's asynchronous and in writing. I am sure we have all found ourselves in situations where conversations and discussions turned stressful, aggressive, petty, or toxic. Without diving too deep into the topic, as it's a big discussion in itself, you can apply much of the advice from *Chapter 1* to make all written communication as nuance-free and inclusive as possible. It's time-consuming to write the first thing that comes into your head without thinking about it, but you will save stress, misunderstanding, and probably time if you do. Of course, this doesn't mean that everyone in a conversation does the same. I have often found that if you try to be as pragmatic, patient, and open-minded as possible when dealing with online communication, you can generally keep a conversation as cordial and productive as possible.

So, when is a feedback round complete so that you can publish changes to the documentation?

This can depend on your work sector and the risk of incorrect documentation. For high-risk sectors such as medical, financial, or industrial, you probably need to have documentation changes fully reviewed and signed off before it's published as mistakes can potentially cost lives or have a large financial impact. In these sectors, software release cycles are also often slower and more considered for the same reason, so documentation releases might be similar.

For most other sectors, there's more leeway. As mentioned several times in this book, much like the software it explains, documentation is never done. It's a constant iterative process of improvement. This means there is a time – often thanks to external pressures such as release dates and marketing campaigns – when you need to close feedback and publish. People tend to get attached to what they worked on and will never be entirely satisfied with the content you've created, but at the same time, if you asked them what perfection would look like, they also don't have an answer. This is all perfectly normal and something you just get used to during feedback. Then, typically, in the hours and days after publishing, you get more feedback that somehow no one had before, and the feedback cycle starts all over again.

Feedback, testing, and maintenance

The previous section covered internal feedback before publishing content. This section covers feedback and usage from your intended users and how to manage that. Getting and processing feedback and metrics on documentation is notoriously difficult. I cover some things I have tried and worked with and things that I know others have tried. However, none of these options are perfect, and the documentarian community is still looking for the "best" way to handle this. There are a handful of ways you are likely to receive feedback on documentation:

- If your documentation is open source, readers and users may create issues about problems they find on the repository for the source of the documentation.

- If the code for the application is open source, users may create issues about problems they have understanding the documentation for the project in the source repository.

- If you add some form of feedback widget (a comments box, a "was this helpful?" option, rate these docs, and so on), then readers and users may leave feedback they have. *Chapter 6* covers some options for this.

- If your product has commercial support via support requests, users may give feedback on the problems and difficulties they find with implementing or using the product. If your product or project has a community forum, then people may post about their problems or experiences there.

While harder to find and generally only suitable for products and projects with a larger user base, you can often find feedback and experiences from the wider community via community-created blog posts, talks, other forums, and so on.

The challenge with almost all of these options is that the feedback you receive may not be relevant to the documentation.

You will probably receive a lot of spam for some of the more public-facing options mentioned previously, such as feedback widgets or repository issues. This includes junk messages and time wasters, especially for larger open source projects, which are full of people trying to increase their online profiles and portfolios by registering tiny change requests or irrelevant comments that don't serve any purpose.

This aside, documentation is often the largest direct interaction point people have with a product, so much like internal feedback, they are likely to use it more as a place to log issues they have with the product. However, this doesn't make it a waste of your time or irrelevant to documentarians. First, feedback on the product is still useful to someone, and you can pass it on to relevant people. Second, it can still highlight areas where documentation needs improvement. If people are frustrated with a particular feature for not working the way they expected or wanted, you may not be able to fix the feature directly or immediately. Still, you can find ways for the documentation to better explain or factor in these frustrations.

Once you have whittled public feedback down to the useful remains, figuring out what to do with it differs from internal feedback for several reasons:

- While valid, one person's feedback from a silent majority of thousands of users may not be worth addressing. If, however, multiple users give the same or closely related feedback, it's worth addressing.

- Opinions and feedback aren't always the same thing. Again, you need to assess the number of people who have given the same or closely related feedback, but remember that someone thinking something is wrong doesn't mean it is.

- Internal roadmaps, priorities, and agendas can trump external feedback and requests. This doesn't mean that you ignore the external input, but it does mean you need to communicate this fact with the feedback giver.

You should prioritize addressing externally contributed genuine errors and mistakes over feedback but still factor in these points when you do so.

But with all these competing feedback items and priorities, how do you decide which to tackle, in what order, and if any changes help? Metrics and measuring the success of documentation is another complex area.

Metrics and measuring success

An obvious place to start is with metrics such as page views, bounce rates, and time spent on pages, but these only tell you some of the story. Is someone spending 30 seconds on a page of documentation good or bad? Maybe they found the answer they were looking for and moved on quickly. Maybe they found nothing and moved on quickly. It's hard to say.

Similarly, what does a lot of page views mean? You might expect that on a getting started guide, but what if there's a traffic spike on an obscure API reference page? What does that show to you? You can build up maps of pathways and assumptions based on traffic sources, search terms, and the pages a user follows, but they won't tell you everything and pure page views aren't that relevant in knowing if documentation was useful.

A more useful measurement option for documentation is tracking how people read pages, and a handful of tools are available. As with many tracking tools, content blockers could render them useless, and if your audience is developers, they tend to be a demographic that uses blockers more than others. But if they do work, they are useful for showing you roughly how a reader scrolls around the page, where their mouse rests, the page elements they highlight, and more. They may not reveal what a reader thinks of your content, but they reveal patterns of usage and provide more insights into the metrics mentioned previously.

A better and more popular metric to track is something along the lines of "time to get started." This tracks how long it takes for a reader to complete a getting started guide. How you set up this tracking depends on your product and its technical stack, but adding interactivity to documentation in different ways is another big topic in itself and one covered later in this book. You can then integrate similar ideas across more documentation pages, helping you track how many people read pages and what they do with the knowledge they acquire there.

Another good metric to try and track is how changes in documentation affect interactions with support. Drawing direct correlations is difficult, and measuring this is a mix of quantitative and qualitative metrics, but over time, you can probably start to see when the quantities of questions relating to certain topics change.

These inputs help you decide what content you need to update and prioritize the order to undertake that maintenance. If you have popular pages that need fixes or updates, then handle those first over pages that see little traffic. Among those popular pages, prioritize the more critical bugs in the content over small linguistic tweaks.

It's good practice to maintain the most popular pages regularly, even if no one has mentioned any actual issues. How regularly you do this depends on the available resources, but you can use some of the metrics sources mentioned previously to determine which pages to cast a fresh pair of eyes over.

When you have that list, you need to decide on the kinds of aspects of the content you should maintain. Here are some ideas:

- Any changes to the company or project style guide since the page was last updated (more on this topic later)
- Software and dependency version updates mentioned in the content
- Follow any technical flows to see if they still work as intended
- Render errors in the live version of a page
- Screenshot updates for any output changes from the application or project

You can keep a checklist or template of each item to check as you work through pages.

Summary

In this chapter, you learned how to kickstart the documentation process and work with others to figure out what documentation means to all stakeholders involved.

The chapter covered the typical process to follow when creating or updating content and what's involved at each stage. Many of the details vary, depending on your internal structure and processes and the nature of the product or project. However, this chapter presented common advice that almost anyone can follow.

If there's one takeaway from this chapter, it's that documentation is almost always in flux and progress. Hopefully, this chapter gave you the skills to keep up with the ongoing process and keep documentation up to date and as useful as possible to readers.

So far, the book has mostly covered principles and theory, which are essential to know as you learn any process in detail. However, as technically minded people, we all know that, while not as important as we might like to think, tools are also an important part of any process to understand. The next chapter looks at some of the fundamental tools you need and how to select which to use from the myriad options available.

6

Selecting the Right Tools for Efficient Documentation Creation

As technically minded people, there's one thing we love to experiment with more than anything: new tools, techniques, and services. So far, I have avoided touching too much on tooling as it can easily become a rabbit hole to fall far into and get distracted by. But before I can move on to other, more advanced tooling topics, it's time to cover the basics.

Let's talk tooling.

This chapter ties together the topics covered so far to highlight and cover what tools help create, facilitate, and manage what you've learned. As you might expect, there are a lot of options, and I don't have enough space to cover them all in detail. Instead, I cover the general principles of each tool's responsibility, highlight some of the most popular or innovative options, and then suggest other options you can investigate.

The chapter covers tools for the following:

- Writing
- Collaborating
- Managing and rendering
- Analyzing and assessing

Before diving into the details, I need to cover the main methods people currently use to create documentation. Historically, say, when my grandfather was creating documentation, this would have also included print and paper. But for the past few decades, this has almost exclusively been done with the help of digital creation tools for output on screens. However, engineers might still read the documentation in print in some risk-averse industries.

The three main methodologies are as follows:

- **Topic-based**: Conforms to industry-wide standards with specific specialized tooling.

- **Docs as code**: Uses traditional developer workflows and tooling. This is the main focus of this chapter.

- **Browser-based**: Uses tools and services in the browser.

Before diving deeper into the main focus of this chapter, let's take a quick look at how they all compare.

Topic-based documentation

One of the older digital documentation techniques is "topic-based." As far as I am aware, perhaps one of the most well-known examples of documentation that uses this methodology is the AWS documentation (`https://docs.aws.amazon.com/index.html`). This technique breaks documentation into discrete "topics" that cover a task.

For example, the Monito Getting Started guide, Which *Chapter 1* started looking at in, in the *Looking at an example* section, could contain the following topics:

- Choose an SDK

- Register an account

- Get an authentication key

- Use an authentication key with an SDK

- Add an SDK to your project

- Make a call with the SDK

And so on.

When displayed as an unordered list, this doesn't show you the unique point of topic-based documentation. Each of these topics is (essentially) a separate file, or at least a separate section in a file, depending on the tool you use. To create documentation, you assemble these individual topics into different output collections for different purposes. One of topic-based documentation's main purposes is content reusability, and often, the teams that use topic-based processes create documentation that people consume in different ways and formats – for example, on a website, in application help, a PDF, or a printed manual. Topic-based documentation means they can use the same individual topics in different places, leading to efficient content reuse or the "write once, use everywhere" principle.

As topic-based documentation is highly structured and often uses formats behind the scenes that are equally as structured, such as **Extensible Markup Language** (**XML**), it tends to be more consistent, has more standard tooling around it, and suffers less from broken links and other structural issues.

This is one of the key differences between topic-based and docs as code. With docs as code, you often need to "assemble your own tooling." With topic-based, you often get it all in one (generally for a fee). Whether you consider this a positive or a negative is largely up to you, your team's skills, and the size of your software budget.

XML has been with us for some time. While many younger folks in technical communities might be forgiven for thinking it's something they would never have to deal with anymore, it's what gives topic-based documentation the rigid, reliable structure that its users love.

XML is famous for its standards and specifications, and probably the most widely used in topic-based documentation is OASIS **Darwin Information Typing Architecture** (**DITA**) (`https://www.oasis-open.org/committees/tc_home.php?wg_abbrev=dita`). DITA defines the XML document type (something important to XML) and the legal markup it uses. The specification is an open standard, but this doesn't mean it's open source. Rather, it's steered by a community of experts who discuss the standard.

Here's a DITA example taken from XML Mind (`https://xmlmind.com/tutorials/DITA/index.html`). I think most of the syntax is clear, and as you can see, it looks a lot like HTML, which has its history in XML:

```
<topic id="docbook_or_dita">
  <title>DITA or DocBook?</title>
  <shortdesc>Both DITA and DocBook are both mature, feature rich,
document types,
  so which one to choose?</shortdesc>

  <body>
    <p>DocBook 5 is a mature document type. It is well-documented
(DocBook:
    The Definitive Guide, DocBook XSL: The Complete Guide), featuring
decent
    XSL stylesheets allowing conversion to a variety of formats, based
on the
    best schema technologies: RELAX NG and Schematron.</p>

    <p>DITA concepts (topics, maps, specialization, etc) have an
immediate
    appeal to the technical writer, making this document type more
attractive
    than DocBook. However the DocBook vocabulary is comprehensive and
very
    well thought out. So choose DITA if its technical vocabulary is
    sufficiently expressive for your needs or if, anyway, you intend
to
    specialize DITA.</p>
  </body>
```

```
  <related-links>
    <link format="html" href="http://www.docbook.org/"
scope="external">
      <linktext>DocBook 5</linktext>
    </link>

    <link format="html"
        href="http://www.oasis-open.org/committees/tc_home.php?wg_
abbrev=dita"
        scope="external">
      <linktext>DITA</linktext>
    </link>
  </related-links>
</topic>
```

On the negative side, and despite the open standards it builds upon, much of the tooling in the space is proprietary and expensive. Many toolset providers are a closed ecosystem, making it harder to integrate with other tools and services outside of that ecosystem. This makes having an open source community around the documentation harder, as contributors need special tooling and knowledge.

Some popular options for writing topic-based documentation include the following:

- **Writerside from JetBrains** (`https://www.jetbrains.com/writerside/`): A new entrant that allows for topic-based docs and a mix of the various methodologies. Its feature set is rapidly increasing, and if you are already using other JetBrains tools, it will feel familiar. However, despite some docs as code influences, its content export options aren't quite as flexible as other tools in that methodology.

- **Framemaker from Adobe** (`https://www.adobe.com/products/framemaker.html`): Framemaker has existed for a long time, and while it doesn't integrate much with many of the tools Adobe is famous for (Photoshop and others), it does integrate with the enterprise tools they are less known for, such as Experience Manager and RoboHelp. If you publish into the Adobe ecosystem, then it's an essential tool.

- **MadCap Flare** (`https://www.madcapsoftware.com/products/flare/`): This is probably the most feature-full option for topic-based documentation, and many of its users are generally positive about using it. It handles many different output types and a plethora of templates to support that output.

- **OxygenXML** (`https://www.oxygenxml.com`): On the rare occasions I've worked with topic-based documentation, this is the tool I've used, mostly as it's the most affordable and isn't tied to an entire ecosystem. It's not always clear which of the companies' many products you should install. But if you're interested in experimenting with topic-based documentation, Oxygen is probably the place to start.

On the complete opposite side of topic-based methodology is docs as code.

Docs as code

This methodology is a loose set of tools and techniques that have generally settled on the overarching name "docs as code" to describe itself. It is what I am most familiar with, what developers like you are most likely to be familiar with, and what I cover mostly for the rest of this chapter and book.

Docs as code aims to follow principles for documentation similar to those of developers. This includes using markup languages in plain text files in a text editor to write, version control to manage collaboration, testing, continuous processes, and more. As a developer, you have probably created documentation using "docs as code" without even realizing it, as it's often the default way many developers create documentation. But for many technical writers, it's a new workflow and tools ecosystem.

On the positive side, the barrier to entry is low for those with development experience. The choice of content creation tool is largely up to each contributor and is often freely available, thus meaning it's easier to have an open source community around the documentation. It's easier to integrate docs as code with a plethora of other tools and services as it is fundamentally "just" plain text.

On the negative side, the barrier to entry for non-technical people is high. Flexible tool choice can lead to analysis paralysis, and largely, there are few hard-enforced standards in "docs as code." In short, the flexibility of docs as code is the biggest positive and drawback.

I cover tool options in the rest of this chapter, but before I do, there's one other methodology I need to cover: writing in the browser.

Documentation in the browser

While topic-based and docs as code are typically local files on a person's computer, many teams create documentation straight into a browser. This could be via a documentation-specific content management system or a wiki-style system, where writers can create links between content items on the fly (the classic example is Wikipedia).

On the positive side, anyone with an account can contribute, and the toolchain is in place, standard, and kept up to date for all users at the same time.

On the negative side, user-installed browser extensions aside, what you're given is what you get, you generally need to pay, and while browser tools are far more powerful than ever, integration options are limited.

Some popular options for writing documentation in the browser include the following:

- **GitBook** (https://www.gitbook.com): A hybrid of docs as code and browser-based, GitBook attempts to combine many of the positives of both into a tool that satisfies team members with different experiences and knowledge levels.

- **Confluence from Atlassian** (https://www.atlassian.com/software/confluence): If you use other Atlassian tools, you may also have access to Confluence. While it's primarily designed for internal documentation, you can also use it for externally-facing content. I never found it the most optimal option for technical documentation, but with a large ecosystem of plugins and integrations, it's a flexible and widely used option.

- **Knowledge Owl** (https://www.knowledgeowl.com): Aimed at less technical products and businesses but nonetheless popular with an enthusiastic customer base, Knowledge Owl focuses on "knowledge base"-style documentation resources.

- **Paligo** (https://paligo.net): Full of features for the entire content workflow, from planning to publication, Paligo also offers multiple integration options to keep developers and developers' managers happy.

I have already presented many options to consider, and I haven't even gotten into the docs as code methodology in any detail yet. So, how do you decide which to use from this dizzying array?

Choosing toolchains and tools

I think tooling should help you with your work and facilitate what you do. As much as possible, it should get out of the way and not dictate how you do what you do. In reality, this isn't always the case, as tooling has certain opinions, and you often choose it because you like (most of) those opinions. If you're starting from scratch with a toolchain choice or are planning to switch, how do you decide which approach to follow or which tools to use as part of that approach?

The key factors to consider in any tools section process are as follows:

- *What is your current team's experience?* What are they comfortable using, what have they used before, and what do they want to use?

- *How standard is what you're considering?* This relates closely to the last point, but it's important to consider what happens when a team changes. If you use something less common or specialized, it could be hard to replace team members.

- *What's your budget?* I love open source and rolling my own tooling, but it's an easy trap to think that means the tooling is "free." With paid options, you offload development and maintenance work to someone else's team. But when you're creating your own tooling, your team has to set up and maintain it. That takes time, probably more time than you think, and also has a potential inherent cost, as it's time they aren't spending on doing their core work.

- *What do you need?* You might think this is the most important point on this list, but I would argue otherwise. While the overall methodology you choose makes a reasonable difference, once you get down to the level of individual tool choice, it becomes less important, as most tools have most features. In the end, decisions usually come down to the first three points.

Considering all those factors, why do I suggest docs as code?

Why docs as code?

Why have I chosen to focus on docs as code? For several reasons. While I have no metrics to back this up, it is increasingly popular in the documentarian community, and a large number of documentation projects starting now and in the past few years are more likely to choose it as their workflow of choice. In certain fields, especially tools and services aimed at developers, it's almost the only process used. The most important reason I focus on it is because this book is aimed at developers, and it's the workflow that most developers will already be familiar with. Even if you have never written a word of documentation, I am almost certain that the process of using some form of text editor and sharing changes with others via version control is familiar to you.

Docs as code follows almost the same processes as, well, code. As I move beyond the basics toward the end of this chapter and into the following chapters, show that automating, testing, and much more are made possible with docs as code.

For the rest of this chapter, I won't keep referring to "docs as code." You can just assume that unless I specifically mention one of the other methods mentioned earlier, that's the method I am referring to.

But let's start with the first component needed. How do you write, and what do you write with?

Selecting and using a markup language

Plain text for documentation isn't quite the same as a "traditional" plain text file. It's not quite as straightforward as lines of text in a `.txt` file. Instead, documentation uses a "markup" language. I mentioned **Hyper Text Markup Language** (**HTML**) in *Chapter 4*, but the markup languages used for documentation are a little different. They're generally simpler.

There are three markup languages worth considering for documentation: markdown, restructured text, and asciidoc.

Markdown

You have probably seen markdown, even if you don't realize it. Created by blogger John Gruber and activist Aaron Swartz in 2004, they designed it as a markup language intended to be easy to read in its source code form.

Markdown syntax is simple but limited. It's a challenge to learn and remember at first, but it quickly becomes natural. This simplicity has led to what is Markdown's most famous problem. While there are attempts at "standards," they are utilized inconsistently, and many "flavors" exist with different markup to bring additions people feel are missing from the "standards." Much of this is because Markdown wasn't necessarily designed for more complex use cases, such as documentation, but as a more general-purpose markup language for the web. This meant that people found ways to extend it to suit their needs instead.

Markdown is well supported by online tools and services, editor plugins, and more. In most developer-focused tools, and many not used by developers, you can expect to write markdown, and there will be features to support it.

While I acknowledge its limitations, due to its widespread support, the rest of this chapter focuses mostly on tools that use Markdown. I will note if a tool also supports other markup options.

Here's an example of Markdown taken from `kilt.io`, a project I do some work with:

```
# KILT Protocol Documentation Website
The KILT Documentation website is built using [Docusaurus 2](https://
v2.docusaurus.io/), a modern static website generator.
Hosted at https://docs.kilt.io
## Installation
```console
yarn install
```

Local Development
```console
yarn start
```

This command starts a local development server and open up a browser
window.
Most changes are reflected live without having to restart the server.
Where to put the code
To add a code example that is executed and tested, add the file to one
of the code sections.
Depending on where the code example is used, the code has to be put
into a different section in the `code_examples` folder.
* Anything in the SDK section -> `code_examples/sdk_examples/src/core_
features/...`
* The workshop -> `code_examples/sdk_examples/src/workshop/...`
* dApp examples -> `code_examples/sdk_examples/src/dapp/...`
* The Staking guide -> `code_examples/sdk_examples/src/staking/...`
```

This results in the following output:

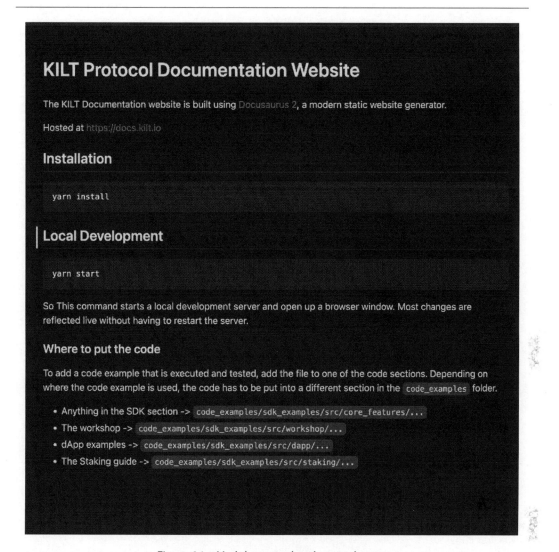

Figure 6.1 – Markdown rendered as a web page

Restructured text

reStructuredText (RST, ReST, or reST) was created by David Goodger in 2001 and is a textual data file format. It's popular in the Python community for documentation.

As RST was designed for documentation, its feature set is more fully realized for that use, with richer semantic markup. Some exceptions aside, it is standard and consistent. However, I have found some syntax challenging to remember and inconsistent with its patterns.

RST isn't so widely supported in tooling and online services, and I have often struggled to find plugins for popular editors that match anywhere near the richness of Markdown options. However, this might have changed since I last looked.

Here's the same Markdown example converted into RST:

```
KILT Protocol Documentation Website
===================================
The KILT Documentation website is built using `Docusaurus
2 <https://v2.docusaurus.io/>`__, a modern static website generator.
Hosted at https://docs.kilt.io
Installation
------------
.. code:: console
    yarn install


Local Development
-----------------
.. code:: console
    yarn start


This command starts a local development server and open up a browser
window. Most changes are reflected live without having to restart the
server.


Where to put the code
~~~~~~~~~~~~~~~~~~~~~~~
To add a code example that is executed and tested, add the file to one
of the code sections. Depending on where the code example is used, the
code has to be put into a different section in the ``code_examples``
folder.
- Anything in the SDK section ->
    ``code_examples/sdk_examples/src/core_features/...``
- The workshop -> ``code_examples/sdk_examples/src/workshop/...``
- dApp examples -> ``code_examples/sdk_examples/src/dapp/...``
- The Staking guide -> ``code_examples/sdk_examples/src/staking/...``
```

AsciiDoc

AsciiDoc is a human-readable document format that was created in 2002 by Stuart Rackham. It is semantically equivalent to DocBook (more part of the topic-based tooling world) but uses plain text markup conventions.

Again, designed primarily for technical documentation, AsciiDoc is packed with markup and features to suit. It is further enhanced by Asciidoctor, a popular addition to AsciiDoc that's so commonly used that it's almost worth considering it a standard part of an AsciiDoc toolchain.

The syntax is somewhere between Markdown and RST. It is more memorable than RST and has similar patterns to Markdown but uses different characters and more semantic markup.

On the positive side, AsciiDoc offers a good middle-ground compromise between features and user-friendliness, and despite its age, it has an active community around it.

On the negative side, while the community around AsciiDoc and AsciiDoctor work hard to provide quality tooling and support to common developers tooling, the support still lags far behind your options when using Markdown.

Here's the Markdown example converted into AsciiDoc:

```
== KILT Protocol Documentation Website
The KILT Documentation website is built using
https://v2.docusaurus.io/[Docusaurus 2], a modern static website
generator.
Hosted at https://docs.kilt.io
=== Installation
[source,console]
----
yarn install
----
=== Local Development
[source,console]
----
yarn start
----
This command starts a local development server and open up a browser
window. Most changes are reflected live without having to restart the
server.
==== Where to put the code
To add a code example that is executed and tested, add the file to one
of the code sections. Depending on where the code example is used, the
code has to be put into a different section in the `+code_examples+`
folder.
* Anything in the SDK section ->
`+code_examples/sdk_examples/src/core_features/...+`
* The workshop -> `+code_examples/sdk_examples/src/workshop/...+`
* dApp examples -> `+code_examples/sdk_examples/src/dapp/...+`
* The Staking guide -> `+code_examples/sdk_examples/src/staking/...+`
```

One feature you might miss from other methodologies is managing metadata around documentation. Fortunately, there is a standard method for doing this: YAML.

Adding metadata to markup with YAML

While you can embed data and variables in addition to text and formatting inline in markup languages through various means, one of the most common is "front matter." This is also mostly always done using **yet another markup language** (**YAML**) syntax at the top of the document. With YAML, you can define a variety of key-value pairs that you can refer to from inside the document or in other tools.

Here's an example of some YAML front matter. It's always placed between sets of three dashes:

```
---
title: My note-taking and knowledge management process updated for
2023
publishDate: 2023-08-25
author: "Chris Ward"
publication_url: https://chrischinchilla.medium.com/my-note-
taking-and-knowledge-management-process-updated-for-2023-
d570ffaf61f0
categories:
  - writing
tags:
  - macos
  - version control
image: "../../../assets/images/articles/1*g4XI5TzcxN4jkorDQ5VUbA.webp"
---
```

To many of you, this all makes reasonable sense. While you might not have encountered all the markup languages I mentioned, you've likely at least come across them. However, markup languages can go further into something that looks a lot more like a programming language.

Making Markdown dynamic with MDX

As I mentioned previously, Markdown is infamous for endlessly adding more flavors to scratch someone's personal itch. Another recent entry to this list is MDX (`https://mdxjs.com`), and I feel it warrants a special mention as a handful of tools I mention later give you the option to use it. What is MDX, and why is it useful for documentation?

The modern frontend world – that is, what people interact with when they use an application through a visual interface – consists of a tree of cascading components. For example, a typical web page might contain a menu component containing menu item components. Below that is a content component containing various other components, and so on.

Conceptually, this is nothing new. Web pages have always basically been made this way. But the way we create web pages behind the scenes has changed. Many frontend tools now break all these page elements into separate files that interact and pass state to each other. One of the most widely used component-based frameworks, and the one that kickstarted this trend, was React (`https://react.dev`), which was created by Meta Open Source.

This is where MDX comes in. It allows you to mix Markdown with components, often React components, but not exclusively. This means you can add all sorts of frontend elements to the Markdown, including some of the documentation-specific formatting options I mentioned in *Chapter 4*, plus many others, including those you use in your actual frontend applications. Even more interesting, MDX also treats content as a component, meaning you can reuse your content or parts of it in different places. I call this new technique and practice "dynamic documentation." Later chapters cover this concept in a little more detail.

The key tools in docs as code

There can potentially be many connected components and tool choices when using docs as code. In this chapter, I present the most fundamental ones, which are as follows:

- **A text editor**: You have to write somewhere
- **Collaboration**: How to work with others, track changes, and maintain a history of work
- **Rendering**: How people will read the documentation

In the following chapters, I look at additional, optional components you can add to a docs as code workflow.

Text editor

It's hard to write anything without somewhere to write. As docs as code deals with what is essentially plain text, there are an overwhelming number of options available to write in. So long as a tool respects plain text, you can use it. This starts to exclude a lot of more common and popular general-purpose writing tools such as Microsoft Word, Google Docs, and so on. These tools tend to mess with a lot of syntax docs as code uses, trying to make it look "prettier" but spoiling the docs as code workflow by introducing elements that other tools later in the process might struggle with. Common offenders are converting straight quotes into "smart quotes," converting Markdown syntax for an unordered list into a rendered list, breaking code blocks, and so on.

For example, quotes in docs as code should be as follows:

"text"

However, tools such as Word and Google Docs convert them into the following:

"text"

In theory, it's possible to change the settings to prevent this behavior, but there's not any reason to as there are far better and more suited tools available, and often for free.

As a developer reading this book, you probably already have a text editor or IDE of your choice. It's probably one you have spent years customizing and configuring just so, and you will defend using it in forums until the day someone forcibly removes it from your machine. The good news is that it is extremely likely you can also use the same tool to write documentation. I won't list all the potential ways you could add plugins and customizations to suit technical writing to every possible text editor and IDE, as each entry could fill a chapter. But suffice it to say that options will be available, and you will find countless blogs giving you recommendations. I even wrote some of them.

I personally use **Visual Studio Code** (`https://code.visualstudio.com/`) and maintain several writing-focused plugins for it. But before that, I used **Atom** (now deprecated) and also occasionally jumped into using **Vim** (`https://www.vim.org/`) and IntelliJ (`https://www.jetbrains.com/idea/`). Despite what many people want to tell you, whatever text editor or IDE you like and want to use will be just fine for writing documentation.

My only caveat regarding this statement is that if you want to use some markup language other than Markdown, it's worth checking how well your editor of choice supports it. Similarly, while less essential, convenience plugins are typically available for many other tools you may choose. If having one of these available is also important to you, then also check if there are options for the editors you are looking at.

Collaboration

I have another piece of good news: as a developer, you probably (hopefully) already use a version control system such as Git or SVN. And docs as code does, too. I always argue that version control designed for code doesn't suit documentation particularly well, which means that documentarians often have to compromise on the writing experience to match developer workflows better.

For example, enforcing fixed line lengths at a certain character length or at the end of a sentence might improve reviewing changes. But it ruins the writing flow and breaks some text-related editor and IDE tools that expect a sentence to flow as it typically would structurally. Often, when correcting documentation, you might change one character, and code-focused version control focuses mostly on the changes made to a line. Despite many documentarians bringing up these issues with version control tool providers, it's unlikely to change, and it's a minor issue that you can often fix with tooling and automated processes anyway.

I don't have much more to say about choosing a version control system or provider since the one you pick will support documentation. Some of the popular hosted services do a better job at rendering files containing markup than others. Most hosted providers also allow people to suggest file changes from within the browser. This is particularly useful if you do end up with a complicated toolchain as it means that people can still suggest small changes without going through a complex setup.

Rendering

One reason plain text markup languages are popular for creating web-based documentation is that they translate cleanly and well into HTML. Tools that handle this process are called **static site generators** (**SSGs**).

What does that mean? It means that the tool takes the Markdown files, plus configuration, theme, and other assets, and outputs a bundle of HTML files or, in the case of some tools, JavaScript files.

Typically, they reflect the underlying structure of the Markdown files, using any folder structure to create a menu structure and the filenames to create paths.

You can then use a basic hosting provider to host those HTML or JavaScript files that any browser can display.

An SSG differs from a **content management system** (**CMS**), which is typically a more complex tool, adding a database and many other infrastructure components to allow for far more dynamism but an equal amount of complexity. The most famous CMS is WordPress. Most CMSs can render Markdown if you use it in a text field, but then you are more in the browser-based approach and not using docs as code. There are tools such as Decap CMS (`https://decapcms.org`) that add a "CMS-style" interface to the underlying Markdown files, allowing you to mix both worlds.

I came to SSGs from the CMS world (Drupal, in my case), and when I first had to use them, I was utterly confused, as they seemed deceptively simple and inflexible. But the beauty behind them is that content and the content creator are truly at the center of the experience. Your content isn't stuck in a database with an enforced creation process. Instead, you can work where you want to and open yourself to the world of docs as code flexibility that I have outlined so far, and there's more to come.

Some SSGs are designed for documentation and others for more general purposes. I recommend sticking with one aimed primarily at documentation unless you have a compelling reason not to, as otherwise, you will probably find yourself endlessly bolting features on that you could have "got for free." Some documentation SSGs are more widely used than others. Typically, the decision is better made by choosing one written in a programming language you, your team members, or your company are most familiar with or already use.

Here's an overview of some of the more common ones.

Docusaurus

Actively maintained by the Meta open source team, Docusaurus (`https://docusaurus.io`) is written in React-style JavaScript. (`https://react.dev`) This makes it modern JavaScript, so it uses MDX, is component-focused, and is a great fit for any modern frontend team. However, modern JavaScript is also complicated, and while it's one of my favorite tools, you can easily get lost in dependency hell and other notorious JavaScript issues. By default, it has several documentation-specific formatting options, including many of those I mentioned in *Chapter 4*, and you can extend them with external components. It supports document versions for different languages or releases, single-sourcing content through components, and the following figure shows a page using Docusaurus:

Figure 6.2 – A page rendered in Docusaurus

Hugo

Written in Go, Hugo (`https://gohugo.io`) claims to be the fastest SSG. It's not designed solely for documentation, but I have come across it used with documentation so often that I'd argue that is what it's mostly used for. I always found its template system confusing when I was trying to achieve something more complex, and I have frequently battled the way it handles automatically rendering menus and sub-pages. These confusions aside, Hugo packs a lot of features for asset processing, output formats, versioning, and a plethora of convenience functions. By default, Hugo doesn't ship with any documentation-specific formatting. Rather, you use Hugo "shortcodes" that you create yourself or get bundled with an appropriate theme, such as Docsy (`https://www.docsy.dev`). The behavior of these shortcodes varies a lot, but you can find ones that help with most of the formatting I mentioned in *Chapter 4*, plus single-sourcing content and much more.

MKDocs

Written in Python, I have always found MKDoc's (`http://mkdocs.org/`) simplicity refreshing, and it rarely disappoints me. That simplicity does mean that it doesn't, by default, do so much, relying on plugins to achieve many of the features other SSGs support by default. However, MKDocs' underlying Python means that you can add standard extensions to its Markdown handling engine, bringing more options. One of the most popular additions to MKDocs is the Material for MKDocs theme (`https://squidfunk.github.io/mkdocs-material/`), which provides documentarians with a lot of helpful functionality, including versioning, but not content single-sourcing, which you need an additional plugin for.

Astro Starlight

I built my own personal website in Astro, and if something such as Docusaurus isn't complex enough for you, then try Astro's documentation option, Starlight (`https://starlight.astro.build`). When I last tested it, the project was in its early days and was missing a lot of useful features. However, if it moves as quickly as Astro, the community will plug those missing features soon. Still, at the time of writing, Starlight includes features for the most common documentation-specific formatting, and you can add many others with external plugin components. It uses some inconsistent patterns for those features, which I found confusing when I last tried it. Astro doesn't use React and instead uses a similar component-based architecture and MDX. Astro also lets you consume content from other sources besides Markdown files, such as APIs, which is one of the reasons I chose it. The following figure shows a page using Starlight:

Figure 6.3 – A page rendered in Starlight

Eleventy

This is another option that's built with JavaScript, and not exclusively for use with documentation, but I know many documentarians who love it, so I've included it as an honorable mention. Eleventy (`https://www.11ty.dev/`) claims to be simple and fast, and it has a friendly community, which helps more than you might think. Much like Hugo, it doesn't include many options for custom formatting; rather, it provides a shortcode framework, and you pick a theme that ships with shortcodes that suit documentation needs, such as plugins (`https://www.npmjs.com/search?q=keywords:markdown-it-plugin`).

Sphinx

Any of you already familiar with documentation tools that use Markdown might wonder why I included Sphinx in this list. Sphinx (`http://sphinx-doc.org/`) is primarily designed for use with RST files but also supports content sources from Markdown and AsciiDoc. However, because Sphinx doesn't add many features and instead leverages those found in RST and AsciiDoc, you do lose access to many features if you use Markdown. So, unless you want to use it for compatibility reasons, it's probably not the best option for Markdown. It's a well-known enough tool, so I thought I should mention it in passing at least.

> **Remember that some people just want to write**
>
> So far, I have only really talked about the positives of docs as code and all the tools that are part of it. If you have development or DevOps experience, docs as code probably don't seem so complex or challenging. However, in the documentation world, you are likely to encounter people who don't have as much experience with those skills. While many of the docs as code tools and processes follow familiar patterns and practices, there is still a lot of initial setup and ongoing maintenance that someone needs to do. The more complexity you introduce, the more maintenance work is needed, and the more custom work you introduce, which means the more likely you are to miss people if they move on from your project or company.

Helping less technical writers with headless CMS

Earlier in this chapter, I mentioned other common methods for creating documentation outside of the docs as code practice, such as using a CMS or wiki. There is a middle ground that's quickly worth mentioning: headless CMS. This method is especially useful for those in mixed teams with other team members who might struggle using text editors, markdown, and version control. Instead, you can mix both, using a CMS to create and maintain content workflow and markdown files. The CMS outputs content as JSON APIs that you can consume in frontend applications to render the content.

Many of the tools in the headless CMS world are commercial, such as **Contentful** (`https://www.contentful.com/`) and **DatoCMS** (`https://www.datocms.com`), but there are a handful of open source options, such as **Strapi** (`https://strapi.io/`) and **Ghost** (`https://ghost.org`), and even traditional CMS that often have some headless mode these days. I am unsure how popular the headless CMS trend still is. Whenever I tested a tool, I found the content creation process relatively smooth, but often, the ingestion side of frontend tools was more complex than it could be.

But headless CMS remains a potential option for those of you in larger mixed companies who want a more cohesive content experience but would still like to take advantage of some of the aspects of docs as code.

Analyzing documentation performance

After a chapter of discussion on docs as code tools and practices, the tools for analysis are not particularly different from any other website. As I mentioned in *Chapter 5*, the trick with documentation is figuring out what you want to assess before choosing a tool.

Analytics tools

There are a lot of potential options for analytics, including **Google Analytics** (`https://analytics.google.com/analytics`), **Matomo** (`https://matomo.org/`), and **Mixpanel** (`https://mixpanel.com/`). And these are just the services I've used. Your hosting provider or tool (if you're not following docs as code) may also provide other additional options. This isn't a book on analytics setup. Each option would probably take at least a chapter to cover. Instead, I cover some general considerations when choosing and setting them up.

Almost all SSGs have variables in configuration by default or via a plugin for at least Google Analytics. The template takes those variables and renders them in the right places for the correct setup. Google Analytics variables are so common by default in SSG themes that it's worth checking them as they could be set to the developer's account, meaning you're sending analytics to someone else's account!

First, consider that much of your (technical) audience probably uses some form of content blocker, which may mean all your carefully constructed analytics setup is largely bypassed anyway.

Next, think about what you want to assess. This consideration isn't any different from setting up analytics on any other website, but the aims of a documentation site are quite different from a marketing or sales site.

If you want to track time to getting started, as I mentioned in *Chapter 2*, think about how you could do that. Is it tracking what an analytics service identifies as an individual from one start point to a finish point and how long it takes them to get there? There may be better ways to track this through code added to your getting started guide. For example, if someone has to register for an access token, the time difference between registering and making a request signifies they have reached the end of a tutorial.

Neither measure is perfect, but my point is that there may be better ways and tools to measure what's important to you. However, this requires you to create custom code and remember that someone has to maintain it moving forward.

Sentiment

In *Chapter 5*, I mentioned the things to consider when using tools that ask readers what they think of your content. What are the options to implement such a mechanism?

You can create your own in your SSG of choice, but you need to consider where you want to store results. Are they emails? If so, how do you search and parse the results? Do you save them to a file or another data source? This is fairly straightforward for most developers, but remember my caveat – someone needs to maintain this over time:

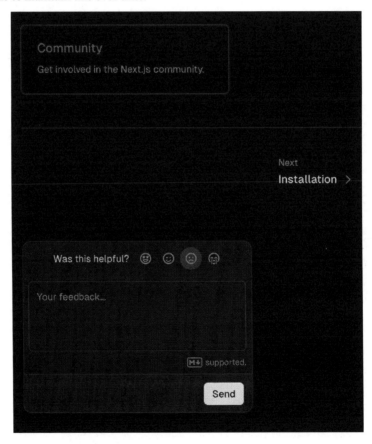

Figure 6.4 – A screenshot of the Next.js feedback widget

Alternatively, you can add a third-party plugin from services such as **HotJar** (`https://www.hotjar.com`), **Usersnap** (`https://usersnap.com`), and **Uservoice** (`https://www.uservoice.com`). But again, remember that many of your readers may block these and never see them.

One last option to consider is accepting feedback directly, where your users are already likely to want to engage and give feedback to you. This is probably in your product or documentation repository. Many SSG templates provide convenience links for readers to suggest changes or provide feedback on a page they're reading. This also means you end up with everything in one place. There are even tools such as **Giscus** (`https://github.com/giscus`) and **Utterances** (`https://github.com/utterance`) that add more user-friendly wrappers around the GitHub API to allow people unfamiliar with it to add comments.

I have almost always worked on open source documentation or tools, but I appreciate this won't be the same for everyone. In this case, most common project planning tools, such as Jira and Asana, also allow widgets that send feedback straight into the tool.

Summary

OK! That was a lot of information and barely scratched the surface of all the options available. Hopefully, you can see that the wide world of documentation tooling, while not quite as wide as developer tooling, offers a lot of options to suit almost all tastes and requirements.

This chapter covered the essential tools you need for using the docs as code methodology while also looking closely at two of the other popular methodologies many documentarians use.

If you want to find more options, take a look at this awesome list for documentation tooling: `https://testthedocs.github.io/awesome-docs/`.

Those essential tools for docs as code are as follows:

- A text editor to write in

- A markup language to use

- A way of collaborating with others

- A way to render the documentation you write

- Methods for assessing how useful readers find the documentation

I also covered important topics related to these tools, such as metadata, newer markup language options, and forward-looking ideas on what documentation could mean. After these essentials, the final two chapters of this book look at these future ideas. As a developer, you've probably started to realize that treating documentation in similar ways to code opens it up to a lot more possibilities than just writing and rendering. And that's exactly what *Chapter 8* is all about. See you there!

7

Handling Other Content Types for Comprehensive Documentation

The last couple of chapters looked at the principles, processes, and tools involved in the process of creating words that form documentation. This chapter covers what else you can add to documentation to help people learn beyond words. It covers the following topics:

- Code examples
- Screenshots, images, and charts
- Animated GIFs and videos
- Interactive experiences

For each of these, the chapter covers what adding those elements brings to documentation, how to add and maintain those elements, and the positives and negatives of using those elements.

We are more than technical writers

I have always had an issue with the term "technical writer," as it implies that all documentation consists purely of the written word.

Many of you have probably heard the following phrase:

"*A picture is worth a thousand words.*"

This may not always be true with documentation, as images aren't always relevant or useful, but the phrase makes a good point. The modern web is generally an all-singing, all-dancing experience, and while documentation needn't go to extremes, you can make it far more interesting than pure slabs of text.

One of the many startling facts you discover about the documentation you invest sweat, blood, and tears into is that people don't pay too much attention to the order of the words you write. They tend to scroll around the page, attracted to elements that stand out, such as images and code examples. *Chapter 4* covered this in some ways, which is why now, in this chapter, I reiterate why it's important to break up walls of text with other elements. As disheartening as it might initially sound, you can use this knowledge to your advantage. You can draw someone's attention with an image or a code example and then gently transition their eyes to the text around those elements containing important information.

With you reassured, I begin with the most common addition to text in technical documentation: code examples to demonstrate concepts.

Code examples

This book is primarily aimed at developers, so I assume that whatever you want to document needs users to create some code. Explaining a technical concept with code examples is one of the more common elements to add to documentation and something readers are used to seeing. They probably expect them. However, rarely are code examples useful or, worse, even functional. How often have you followed a tutorial, copied and pasted a series of code snippets into an editor, to run it and find that it didn't work? I would guess it's quite a common and frustrating experience.

If someone is motivated to learn (or has no choice) your project or product, they will continue experimenting and trying to figure out what's wrong. But they will give up and move on to a competitor if they aren't motivated..If your project is open source, they might create an issue or a pull request. More often than not, you may not even know there's a problem until someone tells you or you try the tutorial yourself.

How and why do code examples frequently end up in such a sorry state? There are a few potential reasons that could include any of the following:

- The writer of the examples made too many assumptions about the reader's prior knowledge and setup. *Chapters 3* and *Chapter 5* covered this topic.

- The code snippets were not written for someone to follow and use but purely as an isolated example.

- It's unclear what a reader should do with the code snippet in the context of a full application.

- The code snippet wasn't tested.

- Dependencies the code snippets use have changed.

I won't address these issues individually but rather review my typical workflow for creating and maintaining good code examples that hopefully reduces as many of these issues as possible. Some steps of the workflow are more straightforward than others, so I will identify which you should definitely do and which you can work on later to improve what you have.

The steps are roughly the following:

1. Decide on a consistent example.

2. Create and organize code examples.

3. Test code examples.

Let's look at each of these steps in more detail.

Deciding on a consistent example

A consistent example is a step in the process that can wait until later. Having the first step as a "nice to have" might seem strange, but there's a good reason for this. It's a good practice to find use-case examples for your code snippets that are consistent throughout the documentation and meaningful to a reader in a real-world way. However, figuring out what these real-world examples could be takes time, especially for new projects or documentation, when you might not be sure what those examples could be.

If you are a developer on the project, then you can probably create those examples yourself. But if you're not, or you're not the **subject-matter expert** (**SME**) on the area you're documenting, you may need help creating those examples, which can also take time.

A place for Hello world

When thinking of adding code to a quickstart or getting started guide, maybe many of you ask, "*Chris, what's wrong with the time-honored 'hello world' code example?*"

Well, nothing, per se. But it's become overused, isn't always relevant or helpful, and doesn't help you pick a consistent example throughout the documentation.

It's better to figure out that example use case first and then think about the equivalent of "hello world." Think of "hello world" as a more abstract concept to think about and show the literal first steps someone needs to take to get something happening with a project.

With all that aside, how do you decide on a use case?

Picking a use case

If you have some ideas after the scoping process outlined in *Chapter 5*, try to align with them as much as possible. As you build in documentation complexity from getting started through deeper tutorials and reference documentation, you should keep the code-example complexity in line to match.

Let's revisit the geocoding example from *Chapter 1* (see – I am practicing what I preach). It's made easier in this case as a geocoding library has a narrower focus than, for example, a programming language, but still, it helps understand how to create code examples with a use case in mind.

How about a delivery service company that wants to use the library to take customers' addresses and convert them to map coordinates so that drivers can quickly navigate to the location to make a delivery?

To begin with the quickstart, you can show the reader how to write code to install, set up, and authenticate with the library and then generate a latitude and longitude pair from an address. That is a good example from which the reader can follow code snippets, run them, and receive a meaningful output.

Then, in other tutorials, you can add more in-depth code snippets that show handling incomplete addresses, routing information, and traffic details. The reference documentation is the one place where you might not need to stick to the example, as an individual **application programming interface (API)** or **software development kit (SDK)** function might be too low-level to remain relevant to the example. Code examples in SDK or API references are also often autogenerated, making adding use cases around them harder.

As you document more complex use cases, you can build upon each example, almost constructing an entire example application or a suite of example applications as you do. This brings us to the topic of how to manage and organize code examples.

Creating and organizing code examples

When you add code examples, one approach is to add them in line with text and other page elements. This is a reasonable approach, but as mentioned in *Chapter 6*, some tools let you create code examples separately and then include them in the documentation. If and when you have time, creating examples as separate example applications brings additional benefits:

- You can test the code. More on that later, and in *Chapter 8*.
- You can provide downloads to let people experiment outside of the documentation.
- Bonus points if you add comments to the downloadable code, as many technical people prefer to learn from reading code.
- Other team members can also use and contribute to this code, such as sales engineers and developer evangelists.

When you create code examples, try to use best practices for the languages and frameworks you show, and use as "real-world code" as possible. It's a fine line as unless you are documenting a programming language or framework, you don't want to spend too long on boilerplate code or the nuances of programming language choice, but you also want to show code that a developer trusts and has confidence in. If you use code that is too trivial or "toy," a reader may not trust the content they read. It connects directly back to the discussion on confident writing in *Chapter 3*. Good technical writing is all about giving a reader confidence in what the documentation says and the product.

However, the step you can take to help improve confidence the most is testing your code examples.

Testing code examples

I mentioned testing code examples in the preceding section, and this is crucial. Test them thoroughly and test them regularly. How often have you come across a code example to find it doesn't work for some reason, directly or indirectly? By directly, I mean the code doesn't work or doesn't do anything, and by indirectly, I refer to issues with dependencies that your code relies on, which is a widespread issue in certain ecosystems.

Testing code examples can take different forms. None necessarily are better than the others.

Manually

The simplest solution is to test manually every time you make changes or at regular intervals as part of a maintenance process outlined in *Chapter 5*. When you do this, play the part of someone visiting the page for the first time. Cast aside your assumptions and preconceptions and imagine the page through the lens of a complete newcomer.

Try to uninstall any already existing dependencies or configurations from previous tests. Depending on the project and its complexity, this can be as simple as deleting any existing working folders or as complex as using tools such as Docker, Podman, or virtual machines to recreate a fresh environment for each test.

Automated

A better approach is to automate testing code examples. There are a handful of ways to do this, and they overlap with other automated processes you already use for developing software, such as **continuous integration** (**CI**) tools. The trick is extracting the code examples to test, and there are a couple of different approaches to this, depending on your toolchain. *Chapter 5* covered documentation toolchains and it depends on which options the tool you use offers for handling code snippets.

One approach is to keep code files separate from the documentation and include or embed them in documentation files. This means you can run, test, and treat the code examples like any other piece of code you work with. But there are some implementation details to be aware of. There's often boilerplate code around the code you want to highlight that's unnecessary to show in the documentation. For example, importing dependencies that the code needs. Sometimes, there are code examples you want to show in the middle of an explanation that you would handle differently in a full implementation.

Another approach is to parse the code examples from documentation and bundle them into a full application. This comes with implementation details that are almost the opposite of the first approach. You must add the boilerplate missing from the documentation that a full application needs to run.

Another approach is to host the code elsewhere in an embeddable editor such as **Replit** (`https://replit.com/`), **JSFiddle** (`https://jsfiddle.net`), or **GitHub Gists** (`https://gist.github.com`). However, these only work for certain languages and move more toward the domain of interactive experiences, which I cover later in the chapter. If you choose this option, it shares many of the same implementation details as the first approach. That is, how do you hide or show the boilerplate code that is unnecessary to show in documentation?

Outside of the tools you use to manage and render documentation, another factor in deciding which option to choose can depend on the programming languages you want to show examples for. Different programming languages have different levels of boilerplate and complexity to run the code.

Keeping an eye on prerequisites

Again, *Chapter 2* and *Chapter 4* covered this, but it is relevant to the complexity involved in running code. As you build and test code examples, remember that people need to run them at some point. The more complexity and dependencies you add, the more information you need to give to people who want to run it. Keep prerequisites and dependencies as simple and language- and platform-standard as possible.

The second most common element you are likely to add to technical documentation is screenshots. Screenshots and other images might be more common than code examples for less technical documentation. The next section looks at how to create and maintain helpful images.

Screenshots, images, and charts

Some people are visual learners, and others aren't, or not as much as others. Images are a controversial topic among documentarians, with equal likes and dislikes.

On the positive side, images have the following, they:

- Can explain a concept more simply and succinctly than words
- Give a reader a confirmation that what they see as a result is the expected result
- Help people whose first language isn't English (or whatever the primary language is) understand what they are reading
- Help show flows, paths, dependencies, or structures that would be complicated with words

On the negative side, images have the following disadvantages, they:

- Are harder than text to keep up to date
- Aren't as accessible as text unless accompanied by good alt text (which is rare)
- Increase page weight unless optimized, which, again, is rare
- If you use any form of version control for managing your documentation (more on that in *Chapter 6*), images and image changes add to repository size and weight
- Can overload a page as much as too much text

Images and text should complement each other, not replace each other. As you write, decide whether an image would help clarify your words. When you add an image, think about whether words help clarify it.

But as this section is about using images, for now, I acknowledge the negatives and assume that you have done the same, concluding you think an image is what you need. Let's start with screenshots.

Screenshots

First, ask yourself again if you need a screenshot at all to illustrate a concept, as getting the balance right is tricky. Often, documentarians start at one extreme of the scale, creating too many or too few and then slowly removing or adding them to reach an ideal amount.

If you are documenting a project that most people interact with via a **graphical user interface** (**GUI**), you may need more screenshots than one that most people interact with via a CLI, API, or code function. However, this is still not completely clear-cut. A good rule of thumb is if something is unclear or open to interpretation from an explanation, then clarify it with a screenshot.

For example, take an application that uses a GUI, which has an important preference that many users miss. You could argue that the application should be better designed, but let's set that aside, as it's not directly our role. In this case, creating a screenshot highlighting the preference in question is worth doing, as the following example shows:

Figure 7.1 – An annotated screenshot (layout) of the Postman interface

However, if an application primarily has a terminal interface, you likely don't need an image-based representation of its output and can use code examples to do the same.

The gray area begins in between these two extremes. If your project relies primarily on a graphical interface, do you create screenshots for every window, menu, and panel? The decision comes down to conversations you have with other stakeholders, how much you follow the operating system or framework patterns for design, and your company's confidence in how complex you think the application is. The potential risk associated with improper use of your application also plays a big factor. If you work in high-risk sectors such as medical or financial, you might want to be cautious and include many screenshots to ensure users follow steps as accurately or as well-informed as possible. With lower-risk software, too many screenshots may give the impression that a project is more complex and needs more explicit explanation than it does.

And when you decide that a screenshot is appropriate and useful, does the screenshot need more? If you create a screenshot to show an overview of the application interface, do you need to annotate or mark areas to identify them? Is one screenshot enough to show an application flow, or do you need to show several with numbered steps?

Do you use real screenshots from your application or what some refer to as a **simplified user interface (SUI)** (https://en.wikipedia.org/wiki/Simplified_user_interface), a kind of pseudo-simulation of what the application looks like?

Slack is a big user of SUI-style screenshots in its documentation. They are often part of an animated GIF, so the following example is taken from one, making it lower quality:

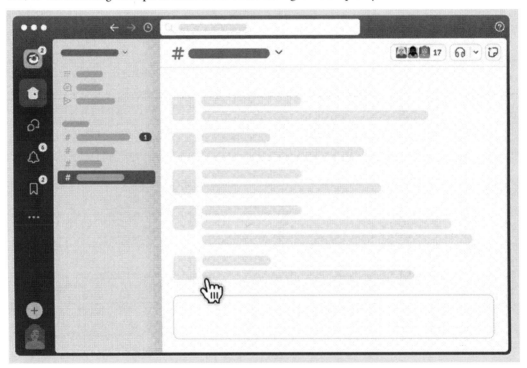

Figure 7.2 – A screenshot of a Slack SUI

And finally, what data do you show in screenshots? Populating screenshots with realistic data is as important as creating realistic code examples. If your screenshots are full of nonsense or inconsistent data, will any reader take them seriously as a useful aid? Where do you get this data from, and how do you populate the application instance you use for screenshots with the data?

Creating screenshots

There are numerous tools for creating screenshots, and they broadly fall into three categories:

- **System default tools** in macOS, Windows, and Linux. These have become far more comprehensive in the past few years, with the ability to add overlays, annotations, crop, and more.

- **Third-party tools** add extra features such as smart removal of interface elements, customizable styles for annotations, and export options. Popular options are the following:

  - **Snagit** (`https://www.techsmith.com/screen-capture.html`) is available for macOS and Windows.

  - **CleanShot** (`https://cleanshot.com/`) is available for macOS.

  - **Flameshot** (`https://flameshot.org/`) is available for Windows, macOS, and Linux.

  - **Shutter** (`https://flameshot.org/`) is available for Linux.

  - **Loom** (`https://www.loom.com/`), is browser-based.

- **Automated options** that borrow technologies from web testing to simulate interfaces and capture their output for screenshots. There isn't really any off-the-shelf tool for this option. It involves hooking tools such as **Puppeteer** (`https://pptr.dev/`) and **Cypress** (`https://www.cypress.io/`) into existing CI processes. This isn't an easy process, but it can be worth it in the long run, as every time you update the interface code, you have new screenshots. I cover some of these ideas more in *Chapter 8*.

Screenshots aren't the only images documentation might need to illustrate a point. Others include flow charts, charts, and diagrams. These can represent myriad ideas, and it's hard to know when one might be more appropriate.

Adding other images

If what you're documenting has a lot of underpinning theory that knowledge of would help people understand better, then consider adding an image of how that theory fits together.

If people often use what you're documenting as part of a complex connection of other components and it isn't obvious to understand, consider an illustration to show how those components connect and relate. Similarly, if what you're documenting consists of multiple components that can connect in different ways and understanding those ways is crucial, consider an image to summarize that.

A good example in the first case is technologies related to Kubernetes. If the project you work on somehow interacts with or extends Kubernetes, then there are often different ways to accomplish this with important subtleties. An image accompanying a text overview could help people understand the differences. The following diagram shows how someone could build a Kubernetes cluster:

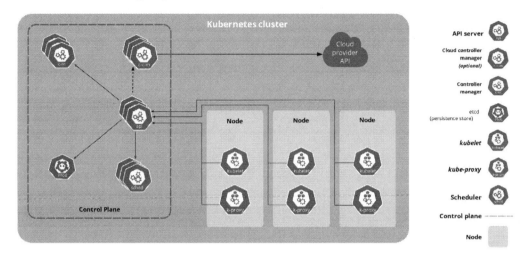

Figure 7.3 – An architectural diagram of Kubernetes

A good example in the second case also crosses over with explaining the theory behind a project. Maybe your project consists of a component that collects data and another that analyzes that collected data. These components are important, so users may want to host and run them on different servers or regions to allow for performance or regulatory issues. Again, an image before the text explaining this could help people understand the possibilities.

The following is another example from the Kubernetes documentation that shows the conceptual history of containers, which is useful to understand when using Kubernetes:

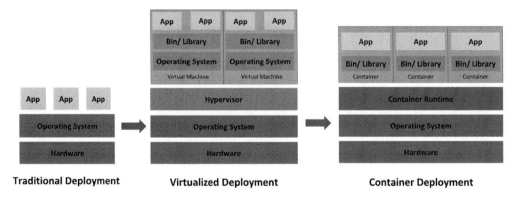

Figure 7.4 – A diagram showing the conceptual history of containers

Finally, charts typically have limited relevance but highly impact those use cases. Charts compare numerical data, so they can show certain concepts far clearer than words. A large list of data is hard for most people to parse and understand, whereas a chart can quickly show that data in the abstract. It misses details but communicates a point across to readers. Marketing and sales teams are notorious for misusing charts to impress people. A classic example is speed charts, which computer manufacturers often use to demonstrate performance increases. They often show a line or bars moving upward with no context or comparison, which is great for selling products but not for explaining them to people. If you decide to use a chart, make sure it's meaningful and purely to inform. For example, it might be to show how upgrading to a new version of a project improves the speeds of some functions over an older version. Or, it could demonstrate how production mode versus debug mode compares.

The following example is from the Eleventy documentation and is a screenshot comparing build speeds between tools:

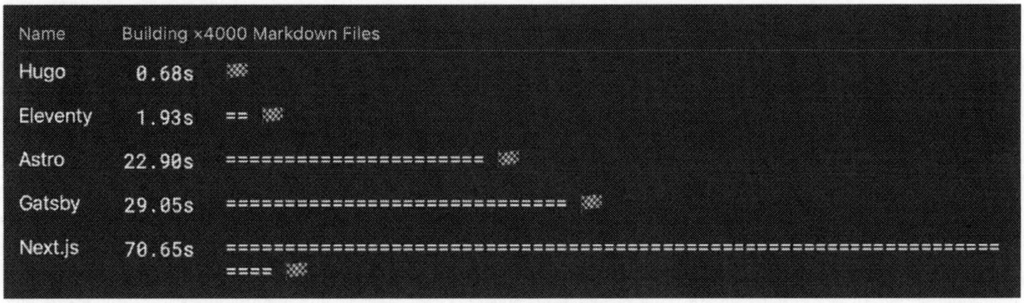

Figure 7.5 – A screenshot comparing build speeds with Eleventy

Making images accessible

A picture may speak a thousand words, but not if someone can't see it. Any image you add needs a way for someone visually impaired to access the content, too. These users often use screen reading applications to help them navigate applications and websites.

At a minimum, you need to add an **alt attribute** (`https://en.wikipedia.org/wiki/Alt_attribute`) to the image that tells a screen reader what to read in place of that image. Technical documentation can be poor regarding alt attributes as many of the tools documentarians use don't prompt you to add them or give much advice on what a good value is. We also tend not to give much thought to what we add to alt attributes, often entering minimal text or, at best, text that describes what the image is; for example, "Screenshot of settings." There are different schools of thought on what you should use for alt tags, but the best answer I heard was that an alt attribute should describe what the image describes. So, in essence, an alt attribute should tell someone who can't see it what you wanted to communicate with the image in the first place.

For example, instead of "*screenshot of settings*," use something like, "*The screenshot shows how to change the text size using the value in settings.*"

If you want to take accessibility a step further, remember my point about images and text complimenting each other. An image added with little context in the text around it may give enough information to someone who can see it, but with no context around an image, even good alt attribute text gives little help to someone who can't see the image.

A final word on adding text-based content to and around images is that, increasingly, humans aren't the only consumers of your content. For many years, search engine crawlers have scraped your text to produce search results, and they also relied on alt attributes to produce context from the images they also can't read. At the time of writing, **large language models** (**LLMs**) are doing the same, as they also can't always understand what's happening in an image. But **artificial intelligence** (**AI**) technology is moving so quickly that by the time you read this, that could be possible. Until that time, however, remember that many entities read your documentation (welcome or not) and can't appreciate the content of images. A picture may speak a thousand words, but it often still needs some to describe it.

Traditionally less common but increasingly popular to add to documentation are animated images or, as they are better known, "videos."

Animated GIFs and videos

A series of images can show the steps someone needs to follow to accomplish a task, but sometimes, it may be easier to show the steps directly. There is also evidence to show that newer learners tend to prefer learning by visual means instead of text. So, for different reasons, a video of some form may be a better method for explaining a concept.

Animated **graphical interchange format** (**GIFs**) and videos share many of the same positives and negatives of images and add more besides. Here is a summary of things to consider.

On the positive side, videos and animated GIFs have the following advantages, they:

- Can show someone the steps to follow and the intended outcome directly
- Give someone the chance to follow along, pausing the video as they do
- Allow for some incidental and anecdotal practical advice while explaining a concept
- Depending on how you create and host a video, it can be more accessible than text with autogenerated transcripts and captions
- Give new learners a format they are more familiar with
- Depending on how you host a video, give a project search optimization, marketing, and discovery opportunities

On the negative side, videos and animated GIFs have the following disadvantages, they:

- Are time-consuming to create and keep up to date.

- Can require specialist equipment to do well.

- Need different skills and experience from what's needed for writing text. Depending on the size and structure of your company or project, it may not be you who creates the videos, but instead someone in marketing, developer relations, or sales engineering. However, as documentation is likely to host them, you should be as involved in the process as possible.

- The creation and management process exists outside of any other tooling you use.

- More experienced learners find it harder and slower to access the information they are looking for.

- Depending on how you create and host a video, it can be less accessible than text for those with low vision or hearing.

Once you have balanced all the positives and negatives of the process and have decided you would still like to make a video of the process, how do you decide what to show?

Tools and processes for video production, editing, and distribution are an entire book in themselves. This chapter covers the general process for creating a video for documentation.

What to make a video of

Generally, videos and those who watch them like to see complete end-to-end processes of accomplishing particular use cases. Ideal candidates for videos are creating versions of getting started guides and tutorials. If you already have the text written, you already have the beginnings of a script. Considering the negatives, it's best to start with your most popular content first and measure the performance of a video before committing to too many.

What to show

Videos do not need to show everything in a process, just the key steps and outcomes. You don't need to show the entirety of progress bars or terminal outputs or wait for processes to complete. The typical length of an instructional video that people might be motivated to watch is around 5 minutes. 10 is considered long. So, for everything you think of including, think if it's needed.

How to record

Without covering tools in depth, the first decision to make is whether you want to include audio and/or video of the presenter with the content you are showing, which is probably a screen share or presentation.

Audio

People want to hear someone explaining what the video is showing. Whoever records this should buy and use a reasonable quality microphone. These aren't as expensive as they used to be and are worth investing in, as anything of reasonable quality lasts a long time. It may sound contradictory, but audio – not video – quality is the first thing people pay attention to when watching a video. Noisy or poor audio irritates people and cause them to move on quickly, wasting any other effort you made. Laptop and phone internal microphones are way better quality than they used to be but use a "proper" microphone, and you instantly notice the difference. Unless you buy a high-end non-Bluetooth model, don't use a wireless microphone as it adds lag to audio and outputs at a far lower quality than a wired microphone. Beyond that, almost any other modern microphone at any price above $30 will probably be enough. If you have the budget, I suggest spending around $100. Anything in that bracket will serve you well.

Without going into too much detail, there are two main types of microphones: analog and digital. An analog or "traditional" microphone uses older cables to transmit its signal. While they often offer better audio quality, you need an interface to translate the signal into a digital signal that a computer understands. You may already have such a device, but if not, then use a digital microphone that connects via a USB cable.

You don't need to set up a professional-grade recording studio (yet). However, try to reduce background noise or excessive echo, which are equally as distracting for viewers and listeners as a poor microphone and are harder to remove during editing. If you aren't a natural public speaker, practice what you'll say before recording and try to sound as confident in delivery as possible, paying special attention to nervous vocal ticks far more apparent in recorded speech than conversational speech. For example, lots of "ums" and "ahs" are acceptable in conversation, but they grate and irritate a listener quickly in a recorded conversation. The same goes for filler phrases and words such as "like," "so," "the thing is," and so on. Finally, watch for non-verbal nervous fillers you add. These include clearing your throat, coughing unnecessarily, smacking your lips, and other actions that listeners notice far more than people you have casual conversations with. You can remove all these in editing, but it adds to the work, and if you also include speaking to the camera footage, keeping things synchronized and smoother is more challenging.

Confident speaking is as important as confident writing for instructional content, and if you don't sound confident, viewers may not trust what they are watching.

That's how to put the words behind what you're showing. How do you show what you want to explain?

What to show

In many ways, the content to consider is similar to the other non-text content presented in this chapter, except that it's dynamic and moving instead of static. If a tutorial had screenshots showing how to accomplish certain steps, that could be a video. If a conceptual guide had charts, you could explain the reasoning behind them. If a getting started guide showed the reader how to build something through code snippets, you could show how to assemble these and construct a working application. In all these cases, the video should focus on what's important on the screen as much as possible. For example, if showing code, make sure the code is readable with regard to font size and contrast. If showing steps through a graphical interface, make sure your mouse pointer and what you're clicking on are visible. Remove as many other distractions as possible from what you are showing, such as notifications, other applications, and distracting background images.

If you are new to making videos, adding footage of yourself is probably something to leave until later, as it adds extra complexity you may not need. As much as documentation readers don't generally care too much about who wrote it, viewers of instructional videos are rarely that interested in who made the video. As you build up a reputation for video content, it might be worth considering adding more "personality" by including your face, but to begin with, it can distract from focusing on what's important: explaining concepts. If you are enthusiastic about cultivating a personality as an individual or a product, it's worth considering adding face-to-camera footage earlier. As with creating good audio, crafting good videos is a large topic, but here are a few small tips to get started.

Hardware is much easier than it used to be. Using a professional camera instead of the one built into your laptop is preferable. These are expensive, and laptop internal cameras are far better than they were even a couple of years ago. However, there are high-grade cameras that many of us carry around all day that are easy to forget. Most modern smartphones upward of about $300 have video cameras capable of resolutions and quality acceptable for creating video footage that can last you well into your videomaking journey. All you need is a screen mount or tripod to position the camera in an appropriate spot for filming.

If you use an iPhone and macOS, then you can use the continuity camera feature to use the iPhone camera with no additional software. If you use other combinations of phone and operating systems, then other options include the following:

- **Camo** (`https://reincubate.com/camo/`)
- **Iriun** (`https://iriun.com/`)
- **DroidCam** (`https://www.dev47apps.com/`)

And there are many others. These are just the options I've tried. The work-from-home shift prompted many similar applications to emerge to suit your budget and feature requirements.

The hardware aside, my two remaining quick tips are to look at the camera as much as possible and to pay some attention to lighting. Looking at the camera is harder than it sounds, as typically, your script or what you're explaining is nowhere near the camera lens. This takes practice, and typically, you need to memorize what you want to say or spend time perfecting your setup to get everything in an optimal position.

Good lighting is almost on par with how a reasonable microphone can lift audio quality. There is little point in using a great camera if you're hidden in shadow. You can improve video lighting by carefully placing lamps and lights you might already own, but LED lights suitable for video making are also much cheaper than they used to be. You can probably buy one or two generic ring lights or rectangular LED lights with stands for a reasonable price that will illuminate you admirably for a while.

Recording

While I barely scratched the surface, for newcomers to video making, that was a lot to take in, and you're likely wondering how to record all this wonderful audio and video you're now ready to make.

Unsurprisingly, there are a few options, and similar to screenshot tools, they range from operating system default to varying price levels of third-party tools depending on your requirements and budget.

Capture

The inbuilt recorders in macOS and Windows are far better than they used to be and now offer reasonably advanced features if you're recording one audio and/or video input at a time. By this, I mean you can record a screen share and microphone or face to camera and microphone, but not at the same time. However, there are certain tricks where you can launch multiple instances of an application simultaneously to record multiple inputs. The system default options rarely offer additional features, such as highlighting mouse clicks, but are fine for your first steps into recording.

The space for third-party capture options is ample, so I highlight some of my favorites and common favorites of others:

- **Open Broadcast Studio (OBS)**: OBS (`https://obsproject.com/`) is free, open source, amazing, and complicated to begin with. But the price and community around it are compelling reasons to try and stick with it. It allows you to create scenes comprising different audio and video inputs to lay out into one output. You could have a full-screen input of your screen, with a smaller overlaid version of your camera over it, plus one or two audio inputs. You can then output that into a recording or, if you feel bold, even a live stream. OBS has a plethora of plugins and extensions and is one of those overwhelming applications, but once you start to uncover its hidden depths, it offers a lot of power.

- **TechSmith Snagit and Camtasia** (`https://www.techsmith.com/screen-capture.html`): While Snagit is more designed for screenshots and Camtasia for video, they both offer some similar features relevant to instructional videos, such as pre-defined layouts for combining screenshare and face-to-camera footage, mouse highlighting, templates for overlays, basic editing features, and more.

Compositing and editing

You can try to capture all your videos in one shoot and remove the need for editing, but this is harder than it sounds, and even then, you likely still need to make small amendments or additions to a video and you need some form of video editor in addition to a capture tool unless your capture tool also offers editing options.

Again, your operating system possibly has some free options, such as iMovie or Clipchamp, which won't offer advanced features but are enough to get you started. For Linux, there's Kdenlive (`https://kdenlive.org/en/`), which isn't built into Linux, but it's a comprehensive option.

If your company has a Creative Cloud subscription, you can use **Adobe Premiere Pro** (`https://www.adobe.com/products/premiere.html`) (my editor of choice, purely because I have a subscription). As with any other professional editing tool such as **Final Cut Pro** (`https://www.apple.com/final-cut-pro/`) or **DaVinci Resolve** (`https://www.blackmagicdesign.com/products/davinciresolve`), they are designed to offer features up to a professional editor level, so they have a steep learning curve. Regarding DaVinci Resolve, Blackmagic Design, the company behind it, now offers its basic version for free, so it is a good option for beginners who want to build up their skills over time.

Interactive experiences

The final non-text addition to documentation is a little harder to define, but it builds upon everything else covered in this chapter. There are certain products and concepts you need to explain that are harder or more abstract for readers and potential users to understand. Maybe it's a new paradigm, or it consists of many interrelated components, or the sheer number of possibilities makes it hard for people to understand where to start.

In these cases, an interactive way of showing concepts can help as it's a way for people to experiment with your product and see results directly. Many people learn by trying and practical experimentation. While code examples people can copy and paste are one aspect of this, they are also a place to lose people as they dive into their text editor and the trials and tribulations of running applications locally. Replicating a way for people to do the same directly inside documentation keeps them inside the documentation. Also, it offers potential methods for gathering metrics on what people learn and how effectively.

What constitutes an "interactive experience" depends a lot on your product or project, as what you need to explain and how it's possible to show vary greatly depending on that. Here are some ideas.

If your project is mostly an API, then the good news is that most API-specific documentation tools include an interactive component. Your main choice is whether to stick with a "mocked" option, where the tool emulates request and response data, or if you want to connect the API to a real backend and return real data.

If your project's main dependency is a programming language, maybe with an SDK, then you're in luck. The options for hosting interactive code examples have exploded in recent years, with everything from platforms that let you embed runnable code snippets to entire editors now available in the browser. Most of the time now, these work with programming languages that need to compile first to run, depending on how niche your compilation target is. However, these only work with browser or browser-like frontend applications. If your intended output is a desktop or mobile application, then while not impossible, showing interactive output is harder.

For projects requiring more components or infrastructure, you can use containers to spin up short-lived demo environments. These containerized environments can contain all your project needs to function, such as databases, caches, other infrastructure, and demo data to show examples of your project in action. The ephemeral nature of these is useful for reducing costs, but when given an environment to play with, developers are likely to try to break it. So, no matter what they try to do, within a few minutes, it's reset anyway. Again, there are a variety of providers in this space, or you can create your own setups.

Adding interactive elements to documentation contributes the most to something I term "dynamic documentation," an encouragement to embrace modern web technologies more in the documentation and benefit from what they can bring. Depending on how you architect what you build, your documentation and applications can share code and data, opening up your documentation to a whole world of potential for you and its readers.

More than final words

This chapter looked at how to explain complex concepts with more than words and how to decide what method works best in which context. The chapter covered code examples, images, video, and interactive experiences and the tools and best practices for creating them. However, you shouldn't feel limited to these media types alone or using only one. The nature of learning and the way people learn is changing rapidly, and anyone charged with helping people understand something must find the most effective learning methods their audience needs and wants.

While not easy to craft, words are relatively easy to create and maintain. Everyone has access to a text editor of some form. A lot of the options I covered in this chapter are a lot more work, and you're probably wanting some advice now to help you save time and work more efficiently. That's exactly what the next two chapters cover. See you there!

8

Collaborative Workflows with Automated Documentation Processes

Chapter 6 covered the tools essential for any documentarian to work with the docs-as-code methodology. But you probably started to realize that treating documentation in similar ways to code opens up many more possibilities for automation, standardization, and testing. While the potential for automating aspects of documentation is vast, this chapter focuses on the following:

- Creating more consistent language with style guides and linting

- Maintaining up-to-date images and videos

- Testing code to ensure it works and is up to date

After these three main topics, it also covers some smaller, miscellaneous ideas.

Striking the right balance

While considering documentation automation, or **documentation operations** (**DocOps**) as some call it, it's too easy to take things too far. You can automate and test so many aspects that the documentation becomes almost as complex as a code base. Documentation is often the first point of call for people who want to contribute to open source projects or a place for less technical team members to contribute things that those with a more technical mindset might have missed. The key to implementing a good balance for automation and testing is to add tooling that helps enhance someone's contributions without blocking them with unnecessary complexity. If someone wants to update a spelling error in a document, should they be required to jump through multiple hoops to do so?

Many of the same code automation and testing rules also apply to DocOps. If tests are unreliable, "flakey," or frequently fail for unknown reasons, are they useful? Testing and automating for the sake of it isn't helpful or constructive. Reducing the amount of repetitive work people must do to ensure quality and consistent documentation is helpful.

Let's begin with one of my favorite DocOps-related topics, which helps everyone in multiple roles and stages of the documentation process: testing style guides or testing for consistent language. But first, what is a style guide?

What is a style guide?

Although *Chapter 3* could have covered style guides, I wanted to save them for this chapter and show you how combining them with DocOps practices makes them more useful.

A style guide is a combination of things, and while many writers have encountered them, developers might be less familiar with them. Think of a style guide as comparable to something such as a configuration file for defining rules for JavaScript code with ESLint (`https://eslint.org`) or Rust with Clippy (`https://doc.rust-lang.org/clippy/`) but for human language. ESLint and Clippy are "linters," and as a developer, you're probably familiar with this code quality improvement concept. Later in this section, I take a style guide and use a linter to enforce it with documentation. This is a practice that is less familiar to writers than developers.

Style guides for human language are nothing new, and while they have existed for centuries in some form, they entered the writing world at scale during the golden age of print media. When you have a publication with multiple writers constantly submitting article copy, you need a way to ensure your publication has a consistent voice. Even though each writer brings personality, they should use similar terminology and phrasing, and all sound like they work for the same publication.

A style guide gathers less obvious rules for how to write. These can include obvious instructions such as using correct spelling or grammar but also areas where different options are possible, and it's a matter of opinion. A style guide could also include the tone of voice, preferred terminology in different situations, how to spell custom branding, formatting, and more.

Different industries generally have different style rules, and some of the most famous and long-lasting are *The Chicago Manual of Style* (`https://www.chicagomanualofstyle.org`) and the *Associated Press* style guide (`https://www.apstylebook.com`), both of which are over 100 years old and are still published and used today.

More relevant to this chapter are the style guides created by several large tech companies that are typically popular among documentarians. These include the *Microsoft Manual of Style* (`https://learn.microsoft.com/en-us/style-guide/welcome/`) and the *Google style guide* (`https://developers.google.com/style/accessibility`), which focus more on writing style rules for documenting software, including guidance on referencing menu items, keyboard shortcuts, and the myriad jargon that fills the technical space.

Typically, a company or project takes one of these style guides to determine most of the rules writing should follow and then adds their own exceptions or additions. For example, I typically use Google or Microsoft and add extra rules for company terminology or areas where the project uses specialized terminology.

So far, so good. Even though human language isn't always as clear cut as code, I think most of you reading can understand why a style guide could be useful for helping you know how to write. However, the style guides presented so far are often large, dry documents, sometimes running into hundreds of pages. Can you really expect someone to consult a document like that every time they write something?

As much as I like style guides, I might expect a professional journalist or humble book writer (!) to follow a style guide. However, it might not be realistic for enthusiastic developers turned documentarians. Style guide documents aren't part of a developer's world. Tools such as ESLint and **continuous integration** (**CI**) are. How can you make a style guide more "developer-friendly"? I am glad you asked!

Developer-friendly style guides

Earlier, I mentioned linters, the tools developers use to enforce style rules for code. It may also surprise you to know that language linters also exist for human language. Mostly English, but some of the tools work with other languages.

Before I move on to the options available, I first want to explain the two main ways these tools work.

The first group of tools typically uses **regular expression** (**regex**) (https://en.wikipedia.org/wiki/Regular_expression), a common tool in a programmer's toolbox for matching patterns. So, for example, if you wanted to check for instances of future tense, you might look for patterns that contain "will" or "'ll". While there are more complex regex techniques for searching around instances of patterns to look for other patterns that might give an idea of context, it has no actual awareness of what you've written. It's just a sequence of patterns.

On the positive, this means tools using regexes are lightweight, can run almost anywhere, don't require communication with a central service, and preserve privacy. On the negative, you end up with many false positives without extensive configuration and tweaking. It's also not possible to turn every aspect of a style guide into code. For example, the Google style guide has a section about not making "excessive claims" (https://developers.google.com/style/excessive-claims). You could check for instances of certain words that people tend to use when making "excessive" claims, but in reality, it's not completely possible to translate to a configuration file or regex pattern. You still need another pair of eyes to check for style guide confirmation in these cases.

The second group of tools uses **natural language processing** (**NLP**) and possibly **artificial intelligence** (**AI**) to detect violations of style rules and consider context. The recent wave of AI tools has expanded the options in this group, but I save covering those newer options for the next two chapters and cover the older NLP-based tools in this chapter. On the positive side, these tools have a better idea of the actual context of writing and can detect some of the more "human" rules, such as the previous "excessive claims" example. I say "better idea" because these tools can still assume a lot incorrectly, especially with technical texts. Because of this, they can offer relevant suggestions to issues instead of broad, uninformed recommendations. On the negative side, you typically have to connect to a service that can run the NLP models, which introduces connectivity and privacy issues and limitations on where you can run the tool. Another negative is also that unless you pay a lot of money, you typically can't customize the rules it uses much beyond a broad suite of general checks. Finally, NLP-based tools suffer from the same issues as the recent wave of generative AI tools. They sound too confident, and people trust their recommendations too much. So, ironically, while they may fix a lot of small grammar issues, they may actually cause more problems with gray-area language than human eyes would notice.

Choosing a type of tool to use

It may not surprise you to hear that which type of tool is best depends.

The regex-based options are more developer-friendly and flexible, so they are better suited to docs as code.

The NLP-based options are better for writing teams consisting of people with different skills and a mix of docs-as-code and non-docs-as-code tooling.

The rest of this section covers a mixture of both tooling options. I personally have more experience with the regex-based tools and actively contribute to one of the more popular tools covered.

Regex-based

In the regex-based tool options, there are single-purpose packages that check a pre-defined set of tools and combination tools that you can configure to check for what you want.

Single-purpose packages

Popular options include the following:

- Write Good (`https://github.com/btford/write-good`) checks for several common style and grammar errors that you can toggle and use via JavaScript, a command-line tool, or IDE extensions.
- Alex (`https://github.com/get-alex/alex`) specifically checks language for some of the unhelpful, offensive, and non-inclusive language mentioned in *Chapter 3*. It's highly configurable, and you can use it via the command line and many other integration options.

You can combine and configure these individual packages and tools, but far more useful are tools that bundle many rulesets and checks together, allowing you to configure the language aspects you want to check. They add initial complexity but offer more options in the long run.

Combination tools

Popular options include the following:

TextLint (`https://textlint.github.io`): If you're familiar with ESLint and the wider JavaScript world, TextLint will feel familiar. After installing the core package, as in the following snippet, for every check you want to add, you install another TextLint package. The following code installs the core package and a rule that checks for any TODO tags left:

```
npm install --save-dev textlint
npm install --save-dev textlint-rule-no-todo
```

You toggle and configure all these optional packages with a `.textlintrc` file in a project or folder. TextLint has a lot of optional packages available (`https://github.com/textlint/textlint/wiki/Collection-of-textlint-rule`) that check everything from grammar rules to markup validation and many of the semantic structural issues mentioned in *Chapter 4*. There are also just as many integration and usage options (`https://textlint.github.io/docs/integrations.html`).

When I first started looking at language linting, I used TextLint. However, it may not suit you if you're not so familiar with the JavaScript ecosystem, and those of you reading who are familiar with the JavaScript ecosystem will notice issues with the approach TextLint takes. Adding lots of single-use JavaScript packages introduces many other JavaScript packages, which in turn introduces many other issues in terms of security, speed, and more. Perhaps the biggest issue is that creating a package to add a check for your custom style rule requires some JavaScript knowledge.

LanguageTool: While the other tools presented in this section are open-source and non-commercial, LanguageTool (`https://languagetool.org`) isn't. Sort of. Some of it is open source, and some of it is free. It's also a tool that has evolved significantly over the past 2 years, meaning that LanguageTool now straddles both the regex and NLP tool worlds. It's usable in many different ways, including offering options for desktop applications and writing tools such as Microsoft Word, which makes it the only option in this section that does and a good choice for those of you working in mixed teams who want to share style guide rules. By default, LanguageTool isn't optimized for checking writing in the markup languages commonly used in technical writing. However, there are in-built and third-party integrations for common text editors and IDEs (and other less technical writing tools) that use LanguageTool, so it is possible to configure and customize it to use with technical writing. The free tier doesn't support custom style guides, but the premium tier does. However, I can't find publicly available details on how to configure those or if it supports standard "off-the-shelf" style guides.

Vale (`https://vale.sh`): This is the tool I help maintain, mostly through the VS Code plugin and contributing to some of the style guide collections. Unsurprisingly, it's the one I know best. The core Vale tool does little, with a handful of in-built checking rules. But through a series of YAML files that define what you want to check for in various ways, which are based on regexes but in a more friendly and flexible way, and a config file, Vale can accomplish a lot in a lean and efficient way. You can build your style guide rules based on existing codified versions of everything from the Microsoft style guide to Write Good to lists of technical jargon words and add your own additions and exceptions.

Test and automate everywhere

The three tools mentioned in this section offer many potential ways to integrate and use them. With great flexibility comes great confusion and the potential to overwhelm you with how to integrate these tools into your workflow. As a keen integrator of language linting tools, I have two main pieces of advice for setting them up.

Tooling workflow

TextLint, **LanguageTool**, and **Vale** all have usage options across the main areas of a documentarian's creative workflow, including an editor, CLI, and CI. To make language linting useful, you should integrate it consistently at every possible stage of this workflow. So, when you are writing in an editor, you should see the same messages as when you push documentation to version control and CI. You could add your own local customizations, but at a minimum, you need to receive what your project has determined as essential checks.

This means that the configuration someone needs to run the tool with consistent checks also needs to be available. Thankfully, as all these tools work well alongside the docs-as-code methodology, this is generally a case of providing a configuration file, much like using any other linting tool such as ESLint. The three tools handle dependencies differently.

For example, Vale maintains pre-packaged style guides as "packages" that you can define in the config file along side where it can find your custom rules, and it then downloads them when run:

```
...
Packages = Microsoft, \
custom-rules.zip
...
```

For TextLint, every style dependency is another `node` package, so you add and install them with a standard `package.json` file.

Then, each integration path, whether editor, CLI, or CI, picks up these dependencies and configurations and runs the same checks, presenting them in a way relevant to the platform:

Figure 8.1 – Vale running in VS Code

Taming results

The other piece of advice is to figure out what checks mean to you and how you introduce them to a team or project without overwhelming people. With all of these tools, you can typically set the error log level for a check to the standard information, warning, and error logging levels.

For example, is a spelling error the highest level of error? What about misspelling or formatting company branding? And how important are grammar errors to you? Should the use of passive voice cause a major error? Or just inform someone of the potential problem? Bear in mind that the check may not be correct due to the nature of checking with regex, especially with technical language and jargon. Often, something that is technically incorrect is, well, from a technology perspective, correct.

Often in CI, the error status also indicates a successful pass of a build or change request, so again, which checks should you allow to fail to block a "pass" status?

Leading on from this, one of the reasons many avoid rolling out a language linter across their entire workflow is because it can be overwhelming. When you first enable some rules and run checks, it typically generates a sea of overwhelming messages that people ignore. I recommend "taming and training" the configuration and text it checks before rolling out a linter widely. This could mean tweaking the rules and correcting errors until you reach a point where the linter only checks new changes. Even then, it's worth considering releasing subsets of configuration until people get used to it. For example, start with error-level checks and add from there.

NLP-based

All of the NLP-based tools are **Software as a Service (SaaS)** models, so the features you get depend on what you pay. Because of this, in the following round-up of the most popular options, I try to include options and plans that include the following features:

- The ability to add custom checks and rules
- API access for more flexible usage
- Variety of editor plugins

There are a lot of choices in this tool space, but here are some I have tried.

Grammarly

Probably one of the best-known language-checking tools, Grammarly (`https://www.grammarly.com/`) has evolved a lot over the years, and like many tools in this space, it now also offers AI text generation (*Chapter 9* covers this in more detail). Any of you who currently use, or have used, Grammarly are probably more familiar with its free and premium tiers, which do a fairly good job of catching various grammar errors. At these tiers, Grammarly has a desktop application that can work system-wide on macOS and Windows, so in theory, it also works in your IDE or text editor. Perhaps Grammarly's biggest drawback is that it's not so good at handling technical copy. For example, code blocks confuse it a lot. Grammarly used to have an SDK, which powered some unofficial extensions, but it will stop working in August 2024, so while Grammarly is great during writing, you can't use it with a CLI, CI, or API, making it limited for docs and code.

At its most expensive tier, Grammarly offers a centralized style guide and brand tone to share among users.

LanguageTool

Yes – LanguageTool (`https://languagetool.org`) gets a mention here too! At its premium tiers, you get NLP-based rephrasing and team-wide custom style guides. Combining this with the open source underpinnings, HTTP API, and many official and unofficial integrations make LanguageTool a flexible option. However, the split between the commercial and open source tooling is often unclear, and I am unsure if the NLP features work via the API.

Acrolinx

One of those companies whose product is used by some of the world's largest companies, although you've probably never heard of it, Acrolinx (`https://www.acrolinx.com`) focuses squarely on large enterprise businesses. Because of this, it's quite hard to get details on prices and features. However, it claims to support documentarians, among others, with support for docs-as-code and topic-based tools (mentioned in *Chapter 7*). It also has a CLI, desktop application, CI options, and more. If you can afford it or can convince Acrolinx to let you test it, it's a comprehensive solution.

ProWritingAid

With a fairly similar feature set to Grammarly, ProWritingAid (`http://prowritingaid.com`) differentiates itself by adding additional features aimed at creative writers, such as an author comparison and writing reports. It has desktop applications, plugins for traditional editors (Word, and so on), and an API at an additional cost. It has style and terminology management, so it is a reasonably priced alternative to other tools in this section, but not so suited to technical writing formats.

Automating image generation

Chapter 7 covered tools for manually generating screenshots of application frontends. I teased that this chapter would cover more automated options to make one of the more tedious processes for documentarians less tedious and more automated.

I wasn't completely honest as there's not actually any "off-the-shelf" tool to do this. Rather, there are options you can try. Someone I know did start creating one that wrapped many of the ideas I cover in this section into something more user-friendly, but he never completed it, and I have tried to open source it but haven't finished the task yet.

In the meantime, like many of the ideas in this chapter, it's a case of taking existing tools aimed more at developers and making them work in the context of documentation. This is why *Chapter 7* suggested following the docs-as-code methodology. As developers, you can apply many of the tools and processes already familiar to you to documentation, too. And some that you're probably already using.

Using test suites

For example, many software automation tools such as Selenium (`http://selenium.dev/`), Cypress (`https://www.cypress.io`), and Robot Framework (`https://robotframework.org`) can generate screenshots. Testers typically use these screenshots to debug errors, but you can also use them to generate screenshots of an application in a known functional state.

Here's an old example I have from when I experimented with Robot Framework and Selenium that takes a screenshot of a particular page element and annotates it:

```
Highlight Form  css=.sessions-form
${note1} =  Add pointy note
...     css=.sessions-form
...     Login here
...     width=250  position=middle
Capture and crop page screenshot  login_page.png
...     css=.sessions-form    ${note1}
```

Any of you familiar with browser automation know that this process involves using CSS or XPath selectors to select elements on a page. This is a challenge, especially in these days of web frameworks that autogenerate classes and IDs on page elements, but with some setup and experimentation, it can work quite well.

You can do similar things with more modern alternatives to Selenium. For example, Cypress has the `cy.screenshot` method. As many application developers use Cypress as part of application testing, you can add the method among testing code at a component level (another concept introduced in *Chapter 7*, showing more relevance), meaning you also don't have to mess around with trying to track down selectors as with Selenium.

Similarly, Puppeteer (`https://pptr.dev`) has the `page.screenshot()` method, but isn't quite as precise, as it's at a page level.

Another single-purpose option is shot-scraper (`https://shot-scraper.datasette.io`), which is purely for taking screenshots, and again, you target areas of a web page through CSS selectors or JavaScript filters. If you don't have time to write more complex test cases or your documentation is too separated from the application code to make it a viable option, it's a good, simple option.

The trick with setting up any of these tools is weighing up the time to implement versus the time you save and configuring where the tool generates that screenshot so that it becomes part of the documentation. And remember that in *Chapter 7*, I also mentioned that with a lot of documentation tools and web frameworks now sharing some of the same underlying tools, you may not even need screenshots anymore. You might be able to embed UI components directly in the documentation instead directly.

Automating other image types

You have a couple of options for images that aren't screenshots, depending on what the image is. For diagrams, there are several popular options for defining "images as code," meaning you can collaborate on them, add to version control, and so on.

Mermaid (`https://mermaid.js.org`) is the best known to developers, and it has good support in many of the editor and documentation rendering tools covered in *Chapter 7*. You define a diagram in a code block, the complexity of which depends on the diagram type, and any tool with the Mermaid plugin enabled renders it as a **Scalable Vector Graphics** (**SVG**) image (an SVG is also code, but quite complex to write and read). Mermaid is fiddly to start with, but as you get near-instant feedback as you tweak diagrams, you can quickly figure out what you need to do:

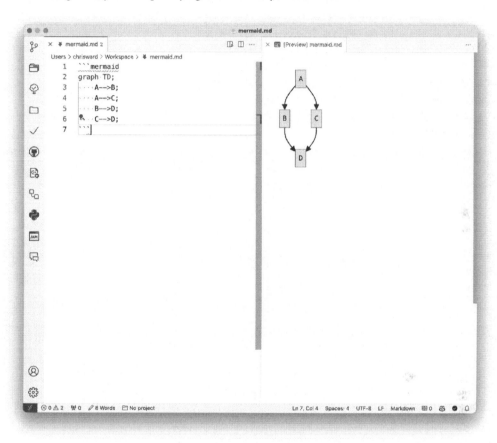

Figure 8.2 – Mermaid syntax and a preview

Before, tools such as Mermaid were in **Unified Modeling Language** (**UML**), and there are still many tools in active development that use its syntax to do something similar to Mermaid, such as PlantUML (`https://plantuml.com`).

Another option is Graphviz (`https://graphviz.org`), which has a syntax similar to that of Mermaid but is a little more complex to render, typically using C code. And finally, Kroki (`https://kroki.io`) is an interesting option that actually wraps all of the options I've presented (and more) to provide a universal API for declaring and, crucially, rendering diagrams from code.

Automating video

Chapter 7 mentioned how many new learners prefer to learn from videos, and the chapter covered some of the lengthy requirements and work needed to create a video. Even once you've created one, they are also hard and time-consuming to keep up to date. Can you automate creating them?

The answer is, as always, it depends. The easiest to automate is any terminal examples. Let's start there.

Converting terminal commands to video

Perhaps the best-known is Asciinema (`https://docs.asciinema.org`). After you run its terminal command, it starts "recording" terminal input and output until you stop recording. You can then either embed that recording in documentation by loading the local recording file into some JavaScript or upload it to Asciinema's site (which is free) and, again, embed it with some JavaScript. You can configure a lot of settings when you generate a recording, but even more interesting is that until you host the recording file with some JavaScript, it's actually a text file. Yes, that's "recordings as code"! In theory, this means you can change the "recording" by editing text, collaborating on it, using it in version control, and so on. Its use is limited to the terminal only, but that might be enough for a lot of application documentation.

Terminalizer (`https://www.terminalizer.com`) is similar, except it saves the recording as a YAML file, and to embed it on a web page, you need to run a command to render the recording as an animated GIF first. So, it's not quite as seamless as Asciinema.

VHS (`https://github.com/charmbracelet/vhs`) is like Asciinema, but it also takes inspiration from the automation tools mentioned earlier, putting the "code" in "recordings as code" foremost. Instead of recording the terminal, you write a `.tape` file (the tool is full of retro references that anyone the same age as me will love) with a series of configurations and steps, then run and output that to a `.gif` file.

Slightly different, newer entrants are tools such as Warp (`https://www.warp.dev`) and Runme (`https://runme.dev`). These aren't technically "terminal recorders" but more tools to share commands and their expected output among teams. Their features for sharing commands into public embeddable locations are new and in development but worth keeping an eye on for a broader knowledge productivity tool.

Other video automation options

But what about non-terminal recordings? Can you automate those? The new wave of generative AI tools offers some options for turning text-based scripts into narration, which *Chapter 9* covers, but what about a video demonstrating a graphical application? At the moment, that's too niche of a topic for any of these tools to handle, but give it time. However, some of the testing automation tools I mentioned in the automating screenshots section also handle video. There aren't too many options, but Cypress (`https://docs.cypress.io/guides/guides/screenshots-and-videos#Videos`)

for web and BrowserStack (`https://www.browserstack.com/docs/app-automate/espresso/debug-failed-tests/video-recording`) for multiple platforms offer some automated video capture features.

Automating code testing

Chapter 9 covered best practices for creating and maintaining functioning code examples and touched on the importance of testing to ensure this. As developers, you likely already have a reasonable idea of the general options available for testing code, but how do you make this work with code examples in documentation? And how do you automate it?

Keep the code separate from documentation and test it mostly as a self-contained application. It may not surprise you that there are advantages, disadvantages, and tools to help while doing this. Luckily, for the most part, it uses tools already familiar to developers.

First, you need to use a markup language or documentation rendering tool that handles the use of file inclusion and, ideally, one with extra features for including code files.

For example, one potentially useful feature is only to import certain lines from a file so that you can hide boilerplate code not useful for an example but needed to test the code. I include those mentioned in *Chapter 4*, but bear in mind that if your tool of choice doesn't support the feature by default, it's probably possible to write a custom component that does.

Both Asciidoc (`https://docs.asciidoctor.org/asciidoc/latest/syntax-quick-reference/#includes`) and reStructuredText (`https://docutils.sourceforge.io/docs/ref/rst/directives.html#include`) support file inclusion by default, meaning that any tool you use on top of them also support it. They also both support partial file inclusion and many other features. It makes you realize why the people who use these two markup languages instead of Markdown are so positive about them!

Docusaurus supports importing code files by default (`https://docusaurus.io/docs/markdown-features/react#importing-code-snippets`), but not partial files, so you would need to find or create a custom component to do that.

MkDocs doesn't allow for file inclusion, but Material for MkDocs does (`https://squidfunk.github.io/mkdocs-material/reference/code-blocks/#embedding-external-files`) and includes options for including partial code files.

Other automation options

Treating documentation as code means you can automate a great deal of things. Here are two more ideas that I have tried.

Converting file formats

When anyone asks, "How do I convert format x to format y?" in the open source and/or docs-as-code world, the answer is almost always pandoc (`https://pandoc.org/`). It's a venerable tool with decades of history and can convert dozens of formats between each other, with a dizzying amount of configuration options. It's a relatively large installation, and if you want to convert to PDF, it also depends on LaTeX (`https://www.latex-project.org/`), another venerable and large dependency. This means it's not always optimal when run in CI systems, but it's not impossible. Also, bear in mind that if you want to use it, convert pages of documentation into formats more suitable for other not-so-technical teams such as marketing or sales; it's possible with pandoc, but you need to factor in how various documentation-specific formatting options will translate.

Accessibility

Chapter 4 covered some ways to make the final HTML-rendered version of documentation more accessible to those using screen readers, navigators, and other accessibility tools. However, how can you ensure you provide the best experience for any of these users? Yes – you guessed it, there's a tool for that: Pally (`https://github.com/pally/pally`). Much like some of the linting tools earlier in this chapter, you provide it with an input, and it returns an error state that you can use to determine if a build should pass or fail. Any issues it finds, you can output as CLI, CSV, or other formats, depending on what you want to do with them. Pally can even launch an instance of a headless browser, meaning you can integrate it more widely with the rest of a testing suite.

Summary

Hopefully, this chapter gave you a lot of ideas to help you reduce the amount of manual work you need to do to ensure consistent quality documentation.

Some of the tools and ideas in this chapter will be new to many of you and not so new to others. But at the moment, we find ourselves facing a major change in new tool options: AI-based tools. Used correctly, these tools can significantly change how you work and write. The next and final chapter of this book looks at those.

9

Opportunities to Enhance Documentation with AI Tools

I am writing this book from late 2023 to early 2024, a time when a new wave of tools and services powered by **artificial intelligence** (**AI**) are disrupting the industry and how people use technical tools. I want to note the date, as it remains to be seen if this is another hype cycle doomed to wane out of our attention or a new paradigm that is truly here to stay.

But at the time of writing, it would be a topic amiss for me not to cover, as when used correctly, these new tools and services have a lot of potential. They have the potential to increase your productivity, bring new ideas and possibilities, and give you time to work on that long list of tasks you "never have time for." They also have the potential to give you incorrect advice, waste valuable resources, and possibly, in the hands of unscrupulous employers, replace you.

There are so many tools and services this chapter could cover, but it would be a long and probably tedious list of links. Instead, this chapter aims to be a culmination of many of the techniques and tooling advice presented so far and how new AI tools can complement those.

This chapter covers the following:

- A brief explainer of the current generation of AI tools and what came before
- Tools and techniques that help you write more productively
- Tools and techniques that help you work with other media more productively
- Tools and techniques that offer new ways for users to interact with documentation
- The technical underpinnings behind these tools and how you can build your own
- Technical and cost implications of these tools and techniques
- Other implications of these tools and techniques

It's a big topic and a big chapter. Let's get started!

A brief history of AI

This is not the place, and I am not the writer to go into any great technical detail on AI. But there has been steady and significant development in AI for decades, if not centuries, and a little history is always helpful in understanding where we are now.

Tools that use AI are nothing new. I studied elements of AI at university in the early 2000s, taught by professors educated in the 1970s. Even back in the 1950s, Alan Turing proposed the "Turing test" (`https://en.wikipedia.org/wiki/Turing_test`), a way of testing for computing intelligence. As with most recent advances in the computing space, techniques and ideas aren't necessarily new, but the speed and scale of operating them are.

The world of AI tools is littered with impressive and confusing-sounding jargon and acronyms that often hide something fairly unimpressive. So, especially at this point in the AI hype cycle, it's useful to unpack some of the terminology you are likely to encounter to better evaluate products.

Understanding AI and ML

AI isn't one technique or technology. It's a broad range of techniques and technologies used to build machines, computers, and software that mimics functions similar to human intelligence. Human intelligence itself is a broad term, but it typically means the ability to process, understand, answer, and react to the input we receive through our five senses.

Machine learning (**ML**) is a subset of AI that gives a system the ability to learn and (hopefully) improve from its experience. In some ways, you could argue that ML is one of the more human parts of AI.

Many tools labeled as AI are actually only using ML, such as shopping recommendations. Most of the language linting tools covered in *Chapter 8* use **natural language processing** (**NLP**). Again, NLP is just one tool in the AI toolbox, but many companies now label long-existing tools as "AI" because that's what the market demands. This doesn't make the tool or service any less impressive or useful, but something that's good at learning isn't necessarily "intelligent."

The problem is that we often don't have a good definition of "intelligence," thus making it hard to replicate satisfactorily. In the infamous words of Deep Thought from Douglas Adams' *The Hitchhiker's Guide to the Galaxy* (I couldn't write a tech book without at least one reference), when asked what the answer to the ultimate question of the meaning of life is, Deep Thought replies (and I am paraphrasing):

"The problem is that you don't know what the question is."

You could spend your entire life studying and working in AI and/or ML and have barely scratched the surface. There are two key technical concepts and advances worth understanding in a little more detail to appreciate the latest wave of tools.

Recent advances in AI

The first advance is **large language models (LLMs)**. Language models are a far older technique of reducing human language to something a machine can understand and use for speech recognition, translation, and more. A "model" in broader AI terms is something trained on a dataset that another tool or service can use to recognize patterns and make decisions on those patterns, typically without human action. So, while a language model is built to work with language, there are also models built to recognize sound, video, and more.

Language models were typically built upon relatively small and specific datasets until the arrival of LLMs around 2017 to 2020. Google's "Transformer", the "T" in GPT (`https://en.wikipedia.org/wiki/Generative_pre-trained_transformer`) proposal in 2017 accelerated the growth and potential of LLMs, increasing their ability to be trained on much larger datasets that often include more general-purpose public datasets. In summary, the recent developments of LLM and Transformer techniques mean it is now easier to ask broader questions to a model and get reasonable answers. It took OpenAI's "chat interface" (ChatGPT), built on versions 3.5 and 4 of its GPT models, to expose these advances to the world. And the rest, as they say, is history.

Of course, while the term LLM is one you've likely heard a lot of recently, many of the new "**generative AI**" (**GenAI**) tools aren't just about text. While there is still a majority of text in documentation, I hope that throughout this book, I have demonstrated that other media has a role in helping explain concepts. This chapter aims to show you tools and techniques that help your productivity across the gamut of topics covered throughout the book.

That said, let's begin by discussing how AI tools can help with the written word and which tools best suit documentarians.

Text and code completion and improvement

Many critics of newer AI tools accuse them of being, among many other things, just a fancy autocomplete. This is a fair criticism, but even the biggest AI skeptic can see that while autocomplete is nothing new, those tools that have adopted these new models and techniques can provide a far better and more informed autocomplete than ever before. The new AI tools have increased context and awareness of not just the last few words you wrote, but the entire document, and depending on the tool, a great many other data points too.

While I mentioned previously that tools now have a broader source of knowledge, writing technical copy is still niche in the grand scheme of things. *Chapter 8* already covered this to some degree in the round-up of NLP-powered (something of the precursor to these new tools) language linting and proofing tools. Almost all the commercial tools mentioned in *Chapters 7* and *8* have added AI features of some description. They work reasonably well for technical copy but don't fully respect the markup formats or the type of language and terminology we use, or know about some of the niche projects we might document.

There are a *LOT* of tools that generate or rephrase text for you, most of which are based on OpenAI's APIs, meaning they all offer fairly similar features and responses. There are almost too many to mention. Some run on the web, some are wrapped in desktop apps, or as part of other tools. Because of this, I try to focus on those that are part of the tools you're possibly already using or are most optimized for technical documentation. But if you want to search for other options, hundreds of blog posts, videos, and other resources tell you about many others you can try. Including plain and simple ChatGPT.

Grammarly (`https://www.grammarly.com/ai`) bundles features for improving structure, voice, and content but also an interesting feature that lets you build your own custom "writing voice."

LanguageTool (`https://languagetool.org/paraphrasing-tool`) offers less comprehensive paraphrasing tools, but I like how it presents the different rewriting outputs in a way that allows you to compare them.

Acrolinx is yet to announce its AI features at the time of writing (`https://www2.acrolinx.com/acrolinx-and-generative-ai`). Their plans seem to involve using your individual content for your own individual LLM, which is interesting and makes sense for an enterprise-focused product.

Those three are more general writing tools, but there are enough AI-powered tools suited to documentarians, some of which you've already seen in this book.

Grazie Pro (`https://plugins.jetbrains.com/plugin/16136-grazie-pro`) is a plugin for any IntelliJ IDE, including Writerside, covered in *Chapter 6*. In addition to the regex-based linting features, the pro version adds AI-powered completion, rephrasing, and translation. Grazie completion isn't quite as smart as some of the other tools, but with a more general AI rollout across other IntelliJ tools (`https://www.jetbrains.com/ai/`), it will likely improve, and if you already use those in your work, then Grazie is a good choice. Grazie doesn't work anywhere else apart from inside the IDE right now, but with a browser extension and browser-based docs feature in progress, it could soon be part of a wider toolchain.

While its public release is recent, GitHub Copilot (`https://github.com/features/copilot`) has actually been in development for some time, and I've had it enabled in VS Code as a tester almost since development began. As Microsoft now owns GitHub and Microsoft has significant interests in OpenAI, it uses a version of GPT-3, as far as I know. Copilot is primarily designed for autocompleting code, but I have found it does a surprisingly good job with text, too. It's trained across all public GitHub repositories and has an immediate context of the repository you're currently working in. It has a tendency to fall into a repetition cycle, output code examples, and, as with many other AI tools, make things up occasionally, but on the other hand, it gets a lot right and has helped save me time on a lot of basic text. If you don't use VS Code, plugins are also available for JetBrains IDEs and Vim.

If you're only interested in code generation, then there are now a lot of AI tools to help. There are so many it's hard to evaluate them against each other. These include the following:

- Visual Studio IntelliCode (`https://visualstudio.microsoft.com/services/intellicode/`), which is also available for VS Code

- Tabnine (`https://www.tabnine.com`), which works with almost all IDEs and editors

- Replit (`https://replit.com/ai`) has its own IDE, but there are unofficial plugins available for others

Generating documentation

One area where things are more interesting is using AI tools to write documentation for you. Throughout this book, I have mentioned tools and ways for automating repetitive and dull tasks. It's all too easy to get excited by the new wave of AI tools as, on the surface, they do some incredible things and can save you a lot of time. They can also sound overly confident and give you output that is not only plain wrong but could cause you problems due to its inaccuracy.

There are two loose groups of tools: for projects based upon explaining something visual and those that involve explaining code.

For more visual application documentation, an AI trawling code or documentation won't generate anything that useful. That is, reading the application code of a website doesn't tell anyone how to use it, and an AI can't generate any useful end-user documentation from the application code. Yet.

Tools such as Scribe (`https://scribehow.com`) instead provide a way of recording the steps for a visual process and then generate documentation for you. None of these tools are very docs as code friendly existing in their own ecosystem, but they do offer export options to formats such as Markdown, meaning that you could still use them to kickstart the process and continue it elsewhere.

On the opposite end are tools that generate comments based on code, typically in an editor or IDE. You can then use these comments to generate reference documentation as mentioned in *Chapter 2*. The inbuilt AI tools in IntelliJ-based IDEs and Copilot in VS Code offer features to generate code comment documentation from the code you select or highlight. From my testing, they both generate different but passable results. There are other IDE-independent options, too, including Docify AI (`https://www.ai4code.io`), Figstack (`https://www.figstack.com`), and Codeium (`https://codeium.com`). There are also tools such as Swimm (`https://swimm.io`) aimed more at internal documentation, a big topic this book hasn't specifically covered, but many of the same principles apply, and you can use it to generate documentation for external users.

AI for audio and video

Throughout this book, I have mentioned ways of creating documentation that don't involve pure text including images, audio, video, and more. Unsurprisingly, there are AI-powered tools to help with these tasks, too. Similar to every other category, there's a lot of choice, and I focus on those that I have used and fit in well with workflows and toolchains you likely already use.

Generating media

Generative AI is well suited for creating images, audio, and video. While many of the tools rapidly appearing in this space are aimed more at marketing purposes, some are better suited to documentarians. They offer some interesting solutions to reduce the amount of time you might need to take to create and maintain content. Again, there are a lot, so I focus on those that are most suited to documentarians and the "as-code" methodology.

Generating images

There are a lot of tools for generating images. The more infamous models and APIs are those such as Midjourney (`https://www.midjourney.com`), Stable Diffusion (`https://stability.ai/stable-image`), and DALL-E (`https://labs.openai.com`). While many have built these models and APIs into other tools, image generation is now so well established Adobe has built it into Photoshop and Illustrator, and Google is starting to offer image generation across its office applications. While all of these are impressive, none are suited for technical documentation, but you may find uses for them.

Generating video and audio

One of the areas where Generative AI can get interesting and time-saving and make video and audio more "as code" is in the rapidly evolving world of generative audio and video. Theoretically, you can write a script and feed it into a system. It outputs AI-generated audio or video you can add in to your editing software alongside human-generated content.

These tools have several issues, but they are worth keeping an eye on. Audio quality has improved drastically from the computer-generated voices you might remember from the past, but it can still have a slight "robotic" quality. Video suffers from the same problem, and as a visual species, "non-humans" still look odd and disconcerting to us, the so-called "uncanny valley" effect. This will improve, and we will also change and become used to it, but more practically speaking, most generated videos are short and expensive to create at the moment. Another practical consideration for both generated audio and video is file format and quality. For whatever technical reason, the output format is generally a lower, compressed format. However, this isn't as much of an issue as with "normally" recorded audio and video, as the footage is pristine and lacks background noise, so it is easier and cleaner to edit.

I also wonder, and possibly fear, that increasingly people won't care. As much as we've become conditioned to low-quality content all over the internet, will we become more accepting of generated media that gives us the answers or feelings we want? The same will probably happen for instructional content. It won't be as perfect or as human as we content creators might want, but if users can get the answers they want in the ways they want, will it matter?

Video

Video generation is much newer, with even OpenAI's Sora (`https://openai.com/sora`) only announced in the weeks before writing, but other tools are already available. Many of them cross over into the feature sets of other tools covered in this chapter, including Canva (`https://www.canva.com/features/ai-video-generator/`), invideo AI (`https://invideo.io/make/ai-video-generator/`), Veed (`https://www.veed.io/tools/ai-video`), and Runway (`https://runwayml.com`). However, Elai (`https://elai.io`) was the only one I could find with an API. None of these are optimal for technical documentation, with most of the non-robotic human output looking kind of like a PowerPoint presentation.

Already mentioned in *Chapter 7*, Camtasia (`https://www.techsmith.com/camtasia-rev.html`) has recently added AI tools, but mainly for layout, background changing, and resizing. Loom AI (`https://www.loom.com/ai`) has many features that overlap with AI-powered editing, which I will cover next, such as filler removal and automatically generating titles, summaries, and chapters. However, showing that it's more of a sales and marketing tool, it can also generate social sharing and **call-to-action** (**CTA**) text.

Audio

Text to speech (**TTS**) is a relatively mature technology but again benefited from recent developments from OpenAI and Microsoft (`https://www.microsoft.com/en-us/research/project/vall-e-x/vall-e/`) to boost quality and speed. These newer advances also allow for "voice cloning"; that is, making a synthetic voice that sounds like a real person. This has a lot of potential negative repercussions, but on the positive, you can also create an automated version of – well, of yourself.

However, this doesn't mean all these tools use those advances. One of the downsides of a hype cycle is that many vendors jump on it and make their products seem newer and cooler than maybe they really are.

If you want to keep things really basic, all the desktop operating systems have TTS in-built, so through a myriad different ways, you could even use those to generate audio files.

Voicemaker (`https://voicemaker.in`) isn't cheap, but it offers an API in addition to its visual tools and a highly customizable feature set for defining tone, emphasis, speed, output medium, and much more. Reflecting its age, most of the major cloud vendors have comprehensive TTS APIs, including Google (`https://cloud.google.com/text-to-speech`), Azure (`https://azure.microsoft.com/en-us/products/ai-services/text-to-speech`), and AWS (`https://aws.amazon.com/polly/`). ElevenLabs (`https://elevenlabs.io`) is one of the newer generations of TTS services, with options for voice cloning, long-form projects, nearly 30 languages, and more.

Editing media

As *Chapter 7* mentioned, editing media is time-consuming. I don't know about you, but I find editing text far quicker than editing audio or video. In my mind, one of the AI tools that has helped me the most in terms of productivity so far has been text-based audio and video editing. The tool generates a text version of your media, and you can cut, copy, and paste from the text version, and it does the same to the media file. Some of the tools also remove "filler" sounds such as "ums" and "ahs," long pauses, and repeated words. On the generative AI side, some of the tools can voice clone based on the text to help fix fumbles or glitches.

I use Adobe Premiere Pro (`https://www.adobe.com/products/premiere.html`), which has recently added many AI editing functions and is rapidly improving its features. Descript (`https://www.descript.com/`), which introduced text-based editing long before the current wave of tools, is an all-in-one editing tool that recognizes people might want to use external tools too, so has a lot of comprehensive import and export options. It also has a rapidly expanding amount of generative features, such as voices, text repurposing of the transcript, and effects.

Not quite an audio editing tool, but audio-related, and worth trying if all you want is a transcript is OpenAI's Whisper (`https://openai.com/research/whisper`). Again, there are a lot of **speech-to-text** (**STT**) tools available now, but I have never found any of them as good as Whisper. For macOS users, I highly recommend MacWhisper (`https://goodsnooze.gumroad.com/l/macwhisper`) for little or no money. It's a fantastic application for quickly and locally transcribing audio from various sources.

There are plenty of other tools that support text-based editing and transcription, but they are part of remote recording tools aimed at podcasters and video makers, not so much for the kind of media designed for documentation.

New ways of interacting

I proposed the idea of a "docsbot" many years ago at a conference when the tech industry was deep in the last wave of "chat interfaces" in 2017/18. The chatbots at the time had very little actual intelligence and were typically large decision trees with a dash of NLP. They were basic and frustrating, but everywhere. In this context, I proposed that users could ask documentation questions instead of clicking through link after link or attempting to find what they were looking for through a search field.

Something like: "Tell me how to install Monito on Linux."

Followed by: "And how do I run it?"

The bot maintains the context you've already provided – the name of the tool and the operating system – and keeps helping you with information relevant to you.

In those days of general frustration with the chatbots of the time, my ideas seemed ludicrous and basically unusable. A few short years later, it doesn't seem crazy, and people are jumping on the idea. If only I'd done something about it then…

In this section, I look at the SaaS options, but there are also ways to create something similar yourself, where I also dig into the costs involved.

Mintlify (`https://mintlify.com`) started as a VS Code plugin for generating documentation from code with AI but has morphed into a more general-purpose documentation platform that I could have also featured in *Chapter 6*. It also now features a chat interface to allow users to ask questions about documentation managed by the platform. **Kapa** (`https://www.kapa.ai`) is probably the best-known independent tool in this space. If you have ever visited the documentation or communities of Netlify, Next.js, or OpenAI, you have seen and possibly used Kapa to ask questions. Mentioned earlier, Swimm also has a chat interface, providing something of an end-to-end documentation solution.

The principles of training and creating your own AI

So far, this chapter has mostly consisted of a lot of services you can look at and pay for to take advantage of some of the forward-looking ideas this chapter discussed. Throughout this book, I have tried to present options that give you as much flexibility and freedom as possible, preferably open source, free, and that give you the option to build upon them sustainably and stably. The current wave of AI tools has a lot of issues, which I cover throughout this chapter, but relevant to the current discussion is that the data sources of LLM-based AI tools are fundamentally different from what you might be used to. The code behind an AI tool might be open source, but this doesn't necessarily mean the model that powers it is. The LLM data model behind an open source tool isn't quite like a database you can potentially dig into and look at. Unless it's connected to an application, you have specialized tools, or the model provider gives you access, the model is generally an opaque black box.

Many of the mainstream AI tools you know and possibly already use, such as those provided by OpenAI (`https://openai.com`), which often feed many of the tools mentioned so far, use general data models. This means that if you want to be able to add a chat-style interface on top of your documentation, powering it with these sources may not be that useful unless your project is a well-known, high-profile project that was used to train these models. Even if it is, then it's likely that the data it contains isn't kept regularly up to date and may refer to sources outside of your control, such as blog posts about your product, and so on.

Earlier in the chapter, I mentioned tools such as **Kapa** and **Mintlify**, but what if you wanted to create your own equivalent that you fully control instead? Bearing in mind what I mentioned previously, is that possible? Yes, it is, but again, it's not quite the same as many of the other open source alternatives I've mentioned in other chapters.

You have two decisions to make. Do you use a publicly available (and possibly open source) model and feed your documentation to it with open source tooling on top? Or do you build everything yourself? Often, even to build everything yourself, you might still need to use non-open tools to do so. While many of the resultant models might be hard to access, many of the tools to train models are free to use and often open source. As I hope is becoming increasingly clear, AI is complicated and not as easy to access or use as other tools in this book.

The simplest option is to use something such as OpenAI's `embeddings` API directly. OpenAI even has a tutorial on creating a "docsbot" you can follow instead of me repeating it here (`https://platform.openai.com/docs/tutorials/web-qa-embeddings`). This process doesn't use OpenAI's models of data but rather uses their models of language understanding. Shall I say it again? AI is complicated! Instead, you use the API to turn your data source (the documentation) into "embeddings," a way of representing text and how different strings relate to each other.

At this point, an aside about cost is useful.

Generally, the pricing model from external AI providers is per token, representing the string you feed into it. So, training and querying depend on the amount of tokens. This isn't as clear-cut as you might expect. One letter or word doesn't equal one token. Let's use OpenAI's pricing calculator (`https://platform.openai.com/tokenizer`) to show some examples:

- "`Hello World`" equals eleven characters and two tokens
- "`HelloWorld`" equals ten characters, and also two tokens, because OpenAI recognizes it semantically to mean the same thing
- "`Hello World!`" is three tokens, as the "!" adds one extra item of meaning

OpenAI states the following:

"A helpful rule of thumb is that one token generally corresponds to ~4 characters of text for common English text. This translates to roughly ¾ of a word (so 100 tokens ~= 75 words)."

Depending on the API settings you use, OpenAI's embedding costs are between $0.02 and $0.13 per 1 million tokens. That doesn't sound like a lot, but the text of the OpenAI tutorial I mentioned previously is about 4,500 tokens. Again, it will add up over time, but creating and maintaining a traditional search index can also cost to process resources or pay for an external service. Using OpenAI's APIs also has several usage limits to bear in mind, meaning you need to "chunk the content" into smaller pieces to stay under that limit, and you need to run the code that does all of this somewhere, which also has a small cost. Querying the new embeddings via OpenAI also has an equivalent cost. However, in a production application, you can use something like a vector database to query, but again, running that database has costs too.

OpenAI's APIs aren't the only option – far from it. LangChain (`https://github.com/langchain-ai/langchain`) is probably one of the better-known options, and it also allows you to choose different model "backends," including OpenAI. Even if you do use LangChain in conjunction with OpenAI, it does a lot of the manual work mentioned previously, such as chunking, for you. Read its chatbot tutorial for more details (`https://python.langchain.com/docs/use_cases/chatbots/quickstart`). Haystack (`https://haystack.deepset.ai`) is another open source option that allows you to connect to different models and many other useful integration points, such as databases and more traditional search tools.

If you want to train your own model in addition to the other steps, then you have many options available. The cost here is the computing resources needed to undertake the training. Training a model based on documentation can run on a powerful machine, including your own, but again, you need to factor in how often you do this.

Unless you have extremely large documentation, training a model on it isn't much work. However, it can still be surprisingly resource-intensive to train and run. For example, Google offers a suite of AI tools you can use at almost any stage of the AI process (`https://cloud.google.com/vertex-ai`). While Google was late to the recent wave of AI tools, they've been working on AI generally for a long time. Hugging Face (`https://huggingface.co`) has hundreds of AI tooling components you can run and use almost wherever you want.

Here's a rough cost and usage example based on some of my experiments using the documentation of a fairly well-known open source tool as a training experiment. The documentation was dozens of pages, adding up to tens of thousands of words at most. I used OpenAI's APIs to create the model, which cost about five or six cents. That's not terrible. Even if you train it once or twice a day, it's affordable. Then, querying that model costs another couple of cents for each query. That, again, doesn't sound like much in isolation, but if your documentation has thousands of visitors per day and even only 10% use the feature, that adds up quite quickly. You also need to factor in that many people will likely mess around with the feature, try to break it, spam it, or generally use it for searches that waste resources.

Multiply these few cents by thousands of users per day, and the cost starts to add up. I have heard from a few people using chat-style interfaces to their docs and similar resources that it can cost hundreds per month.

Is this a lot of money? It depends, of course. The more you optimize, the cheaper it gets. Maybe using these tools reduces your support costs, which are probably a lot more than a couple of hundred dollars per month.

Interestingly, based on trends I've observed over the past few months, many of those projects that started by creating their own "docsbot" switched to using SaaS options instead, switched back to traditional search, or moved bot interfaces away from their websites to community platforms such as Discord. I am not sure why this is, but I can imagine it's because it offers more control and gatekeeping over the usage of these potentially expensive tools.

Writing for robots

All the technical and financial complexities and concerns aside, I think many of you reading this agree that a "docsbot" solves a lot of problems. Creating menu structures that make sense to everyone has always been a challenge for documentarians with a constantly moving definition of success. We add search on top of this to fill the gaps and hopefully allow people to find what they need. But all of this is fraught and non-ideal, as while we organize documentation around our internal ideas of the project or product and how we think people should access it, in reality, all most people want to do is find a way of answering a question they have and possibly don't even fully understand how to ask or what the right answer is. Implemented well, the idea of a "docsbot" that can answer these questions is incredibly helpful and worth considering.

Where is the place for the humble writer in all of this change? Actually, we're better placed than ever. In the medium term, at least. If this chapter hasn't made it clear enough already, the models behind all of these AI tools are content-hungry. They need huge amounts of data to feed them and provide answers. Specifically, they need huge amounts of well-formatted and machine-readable data; that is, content.

Chapter 3 covered advice for good, concise language, and *Chapter 4* covered how to structure content. Both of these chapters hinted at how humans aren't the only ones who read documentation. Traditionally, search engine crawlers might have been smarter than any kind of search you could add to documentation. However, they were still based on the notion of "find this resource for me," and then what you found when you got there, hopefully, in a sea of SEO-generated rubbish, was going to tell you what you wanted to know, and if not, you were back to navigating menus and internal search.

The AI tools now more readily available have far more context about your documentation. *Chapter 8* mentioned regex versus NLP-based tools. Traditional search mostly just looks for patterns. The AI tools have a partial understanding of the content. Actually, they don't really. The "intelligent" part of "AI" is often misleading, but they do enough relational mapping of the content to know how terms relate to each other and when they generally occur, which gives enough context to seem like they understand what you're asking.

This means that more than ever, content needs to follow much of the advice presented in *Chapters 3 and 4*, and you can use the tools from *Chapter 8* to ensure it does. Your good writing makes it possible for these tools to work. It remains to be seen if "docsbot" tools will replace all the other tooling documentarians use fully or partially, but quality content will remain as important for a while yet.

Where documentarians need to be careful moving forward is feeding the machine with content that's also overly AI-generated. Maybe this is more of a problem in the wider world than in documentation, but as we become overly reliant on these tools to help us fill gaps, we risk propagating "truths" throughout the system. You accept one suggestion, and it becomes part of the corpus of knowledge that feeds and answers someone else's question, thus becomes a correct suggestion, and on it goes. generative AI tools are powerful and useful and can help our productivity, but we need to remain in control and always be the final gatekeeper of our own words.

Summary

This chapter covered a lot. In some respects, it could have been an entire book itself, but I hope it provided you with enough topics for further research.

The chapter began with some history and context, dug into tools and services you can pay for, and explained how you might build everything yourself. Throughout the chapter, I also tried to represent the caveats and problems of this growing space. I am not an AI skeptic. I am an AI pragmatist. I think it's a fascinating space, but it's currently so full of hype and nonsense, overwhelming terminology and complexity, that it's important to understand what you're getting into.

That aside, if the recent wave of AI tools is here to stay, they offer documentarians completely new ways to work and provide information to our users. It's easy to fear change, but if your true and prime reason for documenting and reading this book is to help people understand how to use something, and change is what makes that easier for them, then it's hard to resist it.

Index

`packtpub.com`

Subscribe to our online digital library for full access to over 7,000 books and videos, as well as industry leading tools to help you plan your personal development and advance your career. For more information, please visit our website.

Why subscribe?

- Spend less time learning and more time coding with practical eBooks and Videos from over 4,000 industry professionals
- Improve your learning with Skill Plans built especially for you
- Get a free eBook or video every month
- Fully searchable for easy access to vital information
- Copy and paste, print, and bookmark content

Did you know that Packt offers eBook versions of every book published, with PDF and ePub files available? You can upgrade to the eBook version at packtpub.com and as a print book customer, you are entitled to a discount on the eBook copy. Get in touch with us at `customercare@packtpub.com` for more details.

At `www.packtpub.com`, you can also read a collection of free technical articles, sign up for a range of free newsletters, and receive exclusive discounts and offers on Packt books and eBooks.

Other Books You May Enjoy

If you enjoyed this book, you may be interested in these other books by Packt:

Security-Driven Software Development

Aspen Olmsted

ISBN: 978-1-83546-283-6

- Find out non-functional requirements crucial for software security, performance, and reliability
- Develop the skills to identify and model vulnerabilities in software design and analysis
- Analyze and model various threat vectors that pose risks to software applications
- Acquire strategies to mitigate security threats specific to web applications
- Address threats to the database layer of an application
- Trace non-functional requirements through secure software design

Developer Career Masterplan

Heather VanCura | Bruno Souza

ISBN: 978-1-80181-870-4

- Explore skills needed to grow your career
- Participate in community and mentorship programs
- Build your technical knowledge for growth
- Discover how to network and use social media
- Understand the impact of public speaking
- Identify the critical conversations to advance your career
- Participate in non-technical activities to enhance your career

Packt is searching for authors like you

If you're interested in becoming an author for Packt, please visit authors.packtpub.com and apply today. We have worked with thousands of developers and tech professionals, just like you, to help them share their insight with the global tech community. You can make a general application, apply for a specific hot topic that we are recruiting an author for, or submit your own idea.

Share Your Thoughts

Now you've finished *Technical Writing for Software Developers*, we'd love to hear your thoughts! Scan the QR code below to go straight to the Amazon review page for this book and share your feedback or leave a review on the site that you purchased it from.

https://packt.link/r/1835080405

Your review is important to us and the tech community and will help us make sure we're delivering excellent quality content.

Download a free PDF copy of this book

Thanks for purchasing this book!

Do you like to read on the go but are unable to carry your print books everywhere?

Is your e-book purchase not compatible with the device of your choice?

Don't worry!, Now with every Packt book, you get a DRM-free PDF version of that book at no cost.

Read anywhere, any place, on any device. Search, copy, and paste code from your favorite technical books directly into your application.

The perks don't stop there, you can get exclusive access to discounts, newsletters, and great free content in your inbox daily

Follow these simple steps to get the benefits:

1. Scan the QR code or visit the following link:

https://packt.link/free-ebook/9781835080405

2. Submit your proof of purchase.

3. That's it! We'll send your free PDF and other benefits to your email directly.

Made in United States
Troutdale, OR
05/26/2024

20119603R00093